P9-DVC-364

CHARLES PÉGUY

Basic Verities

Mills College Library
Withdrawn

CHARLES PÉGUY

Pierre (handwritten)

Basic Verities

PROSE AND POETRY

Rendered into English by Ann and Julian Green

Mills College Library
Withdrawn

PANTHEON BOOKS INC., NEW YORK

Copyright 1943 by Pantheon Books Inc.
41 Washington Square, New York, N. Y.

Manufactured in the United States of America
American Book–Stratford Press, Inc., New York, N. Y.
Designed by Stefan Salter

FIRST EDITION

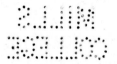

MILLS
COLLEGE

841
P376b

92251

CONTENTS

THE CHRISTIAN LIFE

Poetry

We are aware of the dangers of our undertaking. In Péguy's works there is enough to displease everyone, all the partisans of all parties. For he was severe towards everyone, with a loving, singularly vigorous severity towards those who seemed nearest to him because they encroached on his mystic beliefs: the sternest attacks against the socialist parties date back to his socialistic youth, those against clerics to his Christian years. But what do partisans matter: Péguy is a man who cannot be annexed. For us, promises are sufficiently fine when they come from quarters uncorroded by the corruption of politics. Each sincere party can draw from this precise and ardent dialectic the living germs of rejuvenation. The day will come, and it is close at hand, when one of our greatest poets and a prophetic thinker will be recognized at his true value.

EMMANUEL MOUNIER.

For him also 'the path of salvation is rugged'. It is beautiful and comforting to gaze upon this effort, sometimes rough, always sincere and so profoundly human, that 'shatters old servitudes, overthrows prejudices and idols, and rises little by little towards the light!'

JEAN, CARDINAL VERDIER.

Péguy's style is like that of very ancient litanies. It is like Arab chants, like the monotonous chants of heath and moor; it is comparable to the desert; a desert of esparto, a desert of sand, a desert of stone. . . . . Péguy's style is like the pebbles of the desert which follow and resemble each other so closely, one so much like the other, but yet a tiny bit different; and with a difference which corrects itself, recovers possession of itself, repeats itself, seems to repeat itself, stresses itself, and always more clearly; and one goes ahead. What do I need with more variety! with these loquacious lands which, in the space of a single look and without my needing to turn my head, offer my attention more things than my life can hearken to. I no longer wish to love anything but deserts and gardens; very well-kept gardens and monotonous deserts where the same flower, or one that is almost similar, will repeat almost the same perfume for miles; and the same pebble, the same color and yet each time a tiny bit different; as the Arab flute pipes the same phrase, almost the same, during almost a whole concert; as the believer prays the same prayer during the whole space of orison, or at least, almost the same prayer, with only a trifling difference in the intonation, almost without his being aware of it and almost in spite of himself, beginning all over again. Words! I will not leave you, same words, and I will not hold you quit so long as you still have something to say. 'We will not let Thee go, Lord, except Thou bless us.'

ANDRÉ GIDE.

He had a marvelous gift for stepping beyond the materiality of beings, going beyond it and penetrating to the soul. Thus it is that he knew my most secret thought, such as I have never expressed it, such as I would have wished to express it.

HENRI BERGSON.

His socialism, or more exactly the eminent dignity which he bestowed upon poverty in the world was already the Gospel. . . .

Péguy's socialism was far more akin to the socialism of Saint Francis than to that of Karl Marx.

J. & J. THARAUD.

If he had survived he would have named, numbered and made perceptible, even to the most quarrelsome among us, the resources of France Eternal, all the invisible which helps us, animates us and positively breathes in our blood.

MAURICE BARRÈS.

Péguy is recognized as the poet and representative of his people, because in him, for the first time, the deep silent France of the provinces has found a voice. For the first time since the fifteenth century once more speaks a man of the people, a realist, not one as defined by the savant and man of letters of the nineteenth century, but as a man for whom the deepest spiritual truth is approachable only through the heart and can be grasped only when embodied in the realities of this world.

ALBERT BÉGUIN.

No man was more highly endowed with the peculiar modern awareness of social realities. Péguy sensed the crowd of his class and people round about every one of his thoughts and deeds.—The real world can be, for us, simply an experience of basic verities, a recognition, difficult to attain, of ultimates that are in action, are personal, are impermanently (so far as we as perceptive beings are concerned) permanent.

Indeed it would be difficult for me to express all I have learned to love in him—the tireless searcher to whom more than a few will be in debt forevermore.

GEORGE N. SHUSTER.

A piece of advice in conclusion: read these excerpts aloud. Many willing readers are still inconvenienced by my father's style. To tell the truth, this style is the absence of any style, it is the instant notation of a meditation, of thought at its birth, without the mediation of any art whatever, but this thought is confined and congealed by paper. The living voice alone will restore the richness and movement of life. It is unnecessary that the reading be perfect: it suffices for it to give you a contact with the soul, after which you will no longer lose it.

PIERRE PÉGUY.

Julian Green

CHARLES PÉGUY

THERE ARE so many things to be said about Charles Péguy, in 1942, that it seems difficult to decide how or where to begin. A few years ago, I think that it might have been much easier, I mean that I should have treated him simply as one of France's greatest modern poets, but since the downfall of his country, his name has taken on a new significance. Thousands of Frenchmen have come to him in their present distress, they have come to him for help although he has been dead for twenty-eight years, because they feel the spiritual actuality of his message. He believed in France and died for her on the battlefield of the Marne, and I doubt that any poet has ever spoken for France as he did.

It is always an ungrateful task to try to sum up a man's character in a few words, but in the case of Charles Péguy, much will have been said when we have stated that he was a Catholic and a patriot, because he was one as much as the other and he was both intensely.

Very few races have been as completely misunderstood as the French. This, I believe, is partly their own fault. They

have allowed the world to think that they were gay and pleasure-loving to the point of lightheadedness. They have laughed at everything under the sun as only the Athenians had laughed before them; nevertheless, I have always been of the opinion that the race that produced John Calvin, and Blaise Pascal, and Descartes, and the men of the Revolution, and Pasteur, is as serious as any race that ever walked this earth. But the French do not believe that being serious necessarily means going about with a long face: they have always held laughter as a sort of virtue and, in many cases, an extremely difficult form of courage. There is a saying, in Provence, which, I think, sums up their mental attitude in a few words: 'Le rire dans la rue, les pleurs à la maison', that is, laugh in the street and do your weeping at home. Goodness knows they have cause for tears now, but I should be very surprised if any of their weeping were done in the street.

The fact that French gravity, so clearly marked in French faces, is obliterated for some people by the sound of Gallic laughter, argues a very superficial judgment. Today, the ability to laugh in the face of disaster is one of our reasons for hoping and for believing that France will rise again, because behind this laughter there is the deep seriousness of a great nation.

Charles Péguy was born on January 7, 1873, at Orléans, the city where Bishop Saint Aignan stopped Attila in the sixth century and where Joan of Arc rallied the forces of France nine hundred years later. There was nothing very exalted about Péguy's family. His mother made a hard living by mending chairs, after her husband's death which occurred

when their son was still a baby. Péguy was very proud of his humble origins and when he was a grown man with college degrees and one of the masterpieces of French literature among his manuscripts, he was fond of helping his mother mend her chairs and boasted that he did it as well as anyone in the land. He called himself a peasant and insisted that French peasantry represented what was best in France. When an old French peasant speaks, the race itself speaks through his lips, and the nearer you are to that peasant, the nearer you are to the heart of real France. So reasoned Péguy.

We know very little about his childhood, but the little we know is significant enough. He attended a grammar school at Orléans and went to catechism classes where, apparently, he did very well, for M. Bardet, the curate of his parish, asked him one day if he did not wish to become a priest. The answer was quick and uncompromising: 'No,' said the child, 'that is not what I have in mind.' *

When he was twelve, he was sent to the Lycée at Orléans as a scholarship student, and in 1891, having passed both his baccalaureate examinations, he went to Paris in order to prepare for the Ecole Normale. From what he said in later years, it appears that at this period of his life he had lost all belief in the immortality of the soul. He entered the Lycée Lakanal (at Sceaux, in the suburbs of Paris) and one year later failed in his entrance examinations for the Ecole Normale. Possibly as a result of this setback, he decided to enlist, that is, he joined the colors a year before he would normally have been required to do so.

In 1893, he was free from military obligations and, with the Ecole Normale still in his mind, he entered the Lycée

---

* *'Ce n'est pas mon idée.'*

Sainte-Barbe, one of the oldest schools in Paris and attended in its early days by such distinguished men as John Calvin and Saint Ignatius Loyola. It was at Sainte-Barbe that Péguy met some of the men who were most helpful to him in later times. There was something so compelling about his personality that the more serious of the students in his class came instinctively to him, as if for guidance.

He was on the small side but very robust and a little heavily built. His brown eyes had a way of suddenly flashing when ideas struck him, they were the bold, forceful eyes of a master. His beautiful and delicately formed hands crushed your own in their powerful grasp. When he spoke, there was immediate silence and everyone listened. Why or how this young man of twenty exercised such authority remains as mysterious as genius itself. He was serious to the point of austerity, discountenancing any form of levity such as gambling or drinking, and apparently untouched by carnal desire. There was something of the reformer about him, a gospel-like singleness of heart together with the obstinacy of a peasant and a boundless ability to take pains.

What he spoke of more often was what he called the City of the Future or, at times, the Harmonious City. In the City of the Future, there was to be no more misery, because injustice would no longer exist. There would be no rich people, because only poverty is holy, poverty, not misery, not destitution, as he carefully pointed out, Franciscan poverty, or better, socialist poverty. There would, of course, be no priests of any kind, because in those days, Péguy was an atheist and anything that smacked of religion was extremely suspicious to him. When a man's brain begins to deteriorate, it is as likely as not that he will go back to saying his prayers.

So thought Péguy and so thought his friends who walked by his side, up and down the courts of Sainte-Barbe, building and perfecting the City of the Future with stones made of words.

So completely absorbed was this singular young man by his dreams that he paid little attention to the books that were being written in his day. He read Hippolyte Taine and Ernest Renan, regretting in the latter a senile tendency to believe in God. He knew a large number of Hugo's poems by heart but was never known to have read more than fifteen or twenty of Baudelaire's marvelous lines. On examination mornings, he would ask the student next to him to wake him up in thirty minutes, after he had read the theme of the composition to be handed in. Then he would go to sleep as soundly as a child and upon being awakened would immediately set to work; and exactly on the dot, he turned in a flawless paper which almost always got the highest grade. There was never the slightest mistake in what he wrote and never a correction. Péguy did not believe it was right to make corrections. Whatever went through his mind in connection with the subject was immediately couched in that straightforward style which was already so convincing. Why, he thought, should he turn down a word or a group of words that had come to him as he wrote. They had a right to stand with all the other words on the page. They expressed something in him. He wasn't going to betray them by pretending that they never had been in his mind. So down everything went on the sheet of paper.

There was much of the peasant left in Péguy. In Paris, this heaviness of his marked him as an outsider, a *provincial;* years of Parisian life could never make a Parisian of him,

nor was he at all desirous of becoming what people imagine
a Parisian should be like. His main preoccupation was how
to better the world, how to rid people of their silly ideas
about religion and make everyone a good socialist with no
tommy-rot about heaven or the after-life. Once or twice a
week, he and his little band of friends, you might almost say
his disciples, hunted out the poor at the Butte-aux-Cailles
or at the Glacière and fed them; as many as two hundred
down-and-outs were given warm soup on regular days, but
this act of charity could not satisfy Péguy's ambition: he
wanted to do away with all destitution. At school, he was con-
stantly asking his comrades for money, money for workers
on strike; there was always a strike somewhere and money
had to be obtained immediately; Péguy saw to it that Sainte-
Barbe gave the proper amount. Somehow, it seemed impossible to refuse Péguy anything. He did not beg nor demand,
he merely asked, but it was obscurely felt that saying no to
Péguy was almost as bad as saying no to a saint.

In 1894, he left Sainte-Barbe and entered the Ecole
Normale Supérieure where his old friends soon joined him.
This school, as will be remembered, was founded in 1795
for the training of university professors. There was an atmosphere of intellectual fanaticism at the Ecole Normale
which was exactly suited to Péguy's temper. Generally
speaking, the student body fell into two groups called, in
student jargon, the *talas* and the *antitalas*, the talas being the
believers, and the antitalas the atheists. Sometimes a talas
would share his room with an antitalas and although they
might argue fiercely, they were friends. Thus, in the same
room lived a student, François Laurentie by name, who had
an ivory crucifix on his desk, and a student called Talagrand

who gave himself the proud title of God's personal enemy. Whenever a storm broke out, God's personal enemy would rush to the library and come back with a volume of Voltaire which he read out loud to the accompaniment of thunder and lightning.

Péguy was, perhaps, no less of an atheist, but he must have frowned on God's personal enemy for his lack of poise. He was busy writing a thesis on Kant and social duty and was in as serious a mood as ever. He was also writing something else which he seldom mentioned, the manuscript of which was locked up in a small black trunk; on the top of the trunk, a piece of paper had been pasted bearing these words written in a faultless hand: 'Please do not touch.' The only thing definitely known in connection with the manuscript (which may have been begun at Sainte-Barbe) was that Péguy devoted much time to the study of Vallet de Viriville, who wrote a history of Charles VII, and that he was more and more interested in Joan of Arc.

As time went on, however, Péguy slowly realized that he was not fitted for a university career, probably because he was now conscious of his power as a writer and found it difficult to reconcile the creative urge and the task of teaching. In December 1895, he asked M. Perrot, the director of the Ecole Normale, for a prolonged leave of absence and returned to Orléans with a threefold purpose in mind: to found a socialist center, to learn printing, and to work on his book in more propitious surroundings. By November 1896, at the beginning of the school session, he was back in his room at 'Normale'. But hardly had a few months elapsed when again he walked into M. Perrot's office and asked for another leave of absence. This time, he wanted to

marry. M. Perrot was dumbfounded: examinations were
practically at hand, and here was Péguy asking for leave
of absence to get married. But Péguy insisted that he would
come back and pass his examinations the following year.
'You will fail', prophesied M. Perrot. Nevertheless, Péguy
left school then and there.

The story of his marriage, as told by Jerôme and Jean
Tharaud, who were his school-mates, is so strange that it
would challenge our powers of belief, were it not for our
knowledge of Péguy's unusual conception of moral obligations. It shows how mysterious the most reasonable of men
can be at times.

Péguy had a very good friend called Marcel Baudoin,
also one of his school-mates. We know very little about Marcel Baudoin who seems to have been remarkable chiefly for
his great devotion to the future poet, although the problem
of his influence over Péguy has never quite been elucidated.*
In July 1896, Baudoin died while he was doing his military
service at Dreux, and, as far as one knows, died of natural
causes. Péguy, however, had other views on the subject. To
leave one's friends in this way was a sort of betrayal of
friendship, and Baudoin would never have betrayed his
friends, he must have been killed. By dint of pondering over
this matter, Péguy finally came to the conclusion that Baudoin
had died in consequence of ill-treatments at the hands of a
non-commissioned officer. So one evening he took the train
for Paris and at dawn the next day he went straight to the
house of two of his friends, woke them and said: 'Come, we

---

* M. Marcel Péguy, the poet's eldest son, quotes a written statement of his
father's to the effect that Baudoin actually worked on the first half of Joan
of Arc.

are going to Dreux.' The two friends did not argue. They got up, dressed, and the three men boarded the first train for Dreux. In the train, Péguy explained that he was going to kill the man whom he considered guilty of Baudoin's death. Two swords and two pistols had been brought along for the duel, and Péguy's friends were to be his seconds. They didn't protest or try to reason with him, because they knew that you could no more reason with Péguy than you could with a pyramid. Having reached Dreux, an hour or two later, they made for the barracks and were soon face to face with the man whom Péguy wished to kill. He spoke quietly and it soon became obvious, even to Péguy, that he was almost as distressed as Péguy himself over the death of Baudoin, and just as innocent.

It may have been then that he made up his mind to marry Baudoin's sister in order to take the dead man's place in the Baudoin family. Mademoiselle Baudoin had some ideas in common with Péguy. To begin with, she was, like him, a revolutionary socialist. When he proposed to her, she agreed to become his wife, and in October 1897, they were married. Thus, according to Péguy's mode of thinking, was a grievous wrong partially righted. He was determined that death would not thwart him and that the spiritual link of friendship between him and Baudoin would not be severed. What mysterious logic was at the back of his conduct is difficult to grasp, but we shall see that he did not, even then, consider himself quit of the shade of Baudoin.

In November 1897, we find him again at 'Normale'. At that time, Henri Bergson was teaching at the old school and so were Joseph Bédier and Romain Rolland. The ideas they expressed were discussed as ideas are always discussed by

Frenchmen, feverishly. But apart from that, there were other
causes for excitement in the Latin Quarter at the turn of the
century. Some years before, the Jewish captain Dreyfus had
been arrested on a charge of treason which later turned out
to be imaginary. In 1897, the whole case was to be retried.
It would take many pages to tell about the Dreyfus case.
Suffice it to say that the whole country was being aroused
and divided by the issue at stake, dangerously aroused and
dangerously divided. Some people contended that, even if
Dreyfus were innocent—which they denied—it would be
more expedient to condemn him rather than aspersions to be
cast on a military tribunal and also because certain military
secrets of great importance to the national defense were involved, but there were others, many others, who insisted that,
Jew or no Jew (and that had a great deal to do with it), if
Dreyfus was innocent, he was to be freed immediately. And
of course, Péguy, with his passion for justice, was very loud
in clamoring for the Jewish captain's release.

Péguy had always lamented the fact that he lived at a time
when history had come to a sort of standstill. Nothing seemed
to happen. To use his own words, he was living in a *period*
instead of living in an *epoch*, and that, to him, was a source
of worry and humiliation. He longed for the days when the
heart of France beat fiercely and heroically, as it did, for
instance, in 1793. 1898 seemed absurdly tame and humdrum
in comparison. But now, with an innocent man being accused
of an unspeakable crime, things seemed to be stirring again;
it was like the first mutterings of a terrific storm, and if a
man wished to take shelter, that man's name was not Charles
Péguy. So, wrapped in his long dark cape that made him
look like a pilgrim, with a heavy stick in his hand and his

pince-nez on his nose, he led his friends into the fray. He did what all Frenchmen do when they are really excited, he went down into the street. *Descendre dans la rue,* to go down into the street, is a favorite French phrase. When Frenchmen go down into the street, the world soon knows about it. In 1789, in 1830, in 1848, in 1871, they went down into the street, and now, in 1898, he, Charles Péguy was going down into the street with his friends. A great moment. The end of a period, perhaps, and the beginning of an epoch. And where did they go? They went up and down the Boulevard Saint-Michel vociferating against the 'anti-Dreyfusards'. They marched into cafés where 'anti-Dreyfusards' met. Heavy beer glasses flew in all directions, bottles of fizzy water known as siphons were hurled and exploded, noses bled and countless arrests were made. Péguy took all this very seriously. Had he then used the vocabulary which was to become so familiar to him in later years, he would have said that, by keeping Dreyfus in jail, France was persisting in a state of mortal sin. It was too early for him to speak thus, and yet something was going on in his mind or in his heart; indeed something was always going on in those regions, but this time it was something which even his well-trained Latin brain could not quite fathom.

Perhaps Joan of Arc had a little to do with this. She had always been fond of brave, resolute and stubborn Frenchmen, and here was a Frenchman according to her heart, even though he was an atheist. He might well have fought under her white and blue banner. He was as much of a peasant as she was, and like her, he was not afraid of a broken skull.

During all this time, the manuscript was still in the little black trunk with 'Please do not touch' keeping guard over

it better than any lock could have done, for who would have
dared to open Péguy's trunk? The manuscript was about
Joan of Arc. In fact, it was a drama about Joan of Arc, a
drama divided into three plays. How strange to be writing
a drama about Joan of Arc at a time where people's preoccupations were of the coming revolution, particularly when one
thought of oneself as a revolutionist! But the most self-
conscious among us are capable of delusions about their real
nature. The play was completed in 1897, and its title made
known to Péguy's admirers. A chill of disappointment must
have run down their backs. Joan of Arc! A fifteenth-century
saint chockfull of visions and old-fashioned ideas about
right and wrong . . . They were even more disconcerted when
they were allowed to read the play. Nevertheless it was
Péguy's book, and that was enough. What Péguy did was all
right. Now came the almost impossible task of having the
book published. Péguy had no money and the then enormous
sum of two thousand francs had to be raised. Péguy assem-
bled his friends and explained. They didn't argue, they didn't
refuse, because Péguy's most unreasonable requests could
not be refused and in December of that year the book was
printed. Its size alone was impressive: an octavo numbering
seven hundred and fifty-two pages. As for the chances of
producing such a play on the stage, they were as slight as
the play was long; it would have taken the better part of a
whole day to give it. Very characteristic of Péguy was his
insisting on having a list printed at the back of the book with
the names of all the men who had taken a part in the manu-
facturing of this ponderous volume: printers, readers, cor-
rectors, compositors. What bothered him most was that he
had not been able to find out the names of the men who had

actually made the metal characters and those who had fished out of trash cans the rags used in making the paper. Eight hundred copies were deposited in a socialist bookstore, where they peacefully went to sleep. Then, after many weeks, something happened which startled everyone: a copy was sold.

One of the oddest features of this work was the large number of blanks left in the text. These, Péguy explained, were to be filled in later, but he failed to say how. Such as it is, the drama is little read nowadays, probably because it has been superseded by the Joan of Arc which Péguy wrote in later years. 'I could write about Joan of Arc for twenty years', he once said. As a matter of fact, he wrote about her fifteen or sixteen years of his life. His first Joan of Arc, in spite of its awkwardness and its tendency to stand still when we should expect it to go ahead, is a very moving play, partly because of Joan of Arc whose story is faithfully told, partly because of Péguy whose genius is already recognizable. Even though we are too often reminded of a carefully written school composition, it is undeniable that a tremendous personality is foreshadowed.

As has before been hinted, it would be going too far to say that, when this first Joan of Arc was published, Péguy was already a Christian, although even a not very intuitive observer might have sensed that a complete change of heart was bound to take place in Péguy, sooner or later. Péguy himself was most probably unaware of this. As late as 1905, he refused to print such a hackneyed phrase as: 'God grant that such and such a thing may happen,' because of its Christian, or at any rate, theistic implications, and it was not until 1908 that he declared himself a Catholic. Nevertheless, the fact remains that he chose Joan of Arc as the subject

92251

of his first book, the first part of which, at least, reads like a mystical poem on human suffering and salvation. We are still very much in the dark as to the psychology of conversions. When and how is a conversion brought about? In the case of Péguy, I am somewhat of the opinion that he was providentially influenced by his own work. He had not yet written what lay deepest in him—what lies deepest in us is very often beyond our ken until we go through the struggle to express it, and then it begins to react on us—but in the early scenes of this first Joan of Arc, he comes very close to a personal experience of Christian spirituality. And then, broadly speaking, a man who loves Saint Francis and Joan of Arc as he did and who, moreover, delights in feeding the poor, is a Christian whether he knows it or not.

One has the impression, when reading about Péguy's spiritual difficulties, that as early as 1897 he had an inkling of the crisis to come and that he instinctively shrank from it —instinctively but not consciously—as we are all apt to do when we feel that new problems are about to complicate our lives. There were plenty of complications in store for Péguy. To begin with, the socialist revolution had to be brought about. Also, the daily bread had to be earned. Many plans were agitated. Finally, it was decided that a socialist bookshop would be opened with the financial help of Madame Péguy who owned the then rather large sum of 40,000 francs. A store was found and the bookshop solemnly inaugurated in the spring of 1898, May 1st, the day of leftist demonstrations being, of course, chosen as the date of that event.

Four months later, Péguy who was then completing his third year at 'Normale', failed at his final examinations,

exactly as M. Perrot had predicted, and abandoned all plans for a university career.

To go back to the bookshop, it was situated in the heart of the Latin Quarter, only a few steps from the Panthéon, in the rue Cujas. It was very small and always very crowded, not, alas, by people who came to buy books, but by people who came in to talk, to discuss the Dreyfus case or the coming revolution, that famous 'Grand Soir' which was perpetually casting its lurid glow over the conversations of those days, or that equally famous Grand Sweeping Up, 'le Grand Coup de Balai' which I have heard of ever since I was a boy, but have yet to witness. Such as it was, Péguy thought of his little bookshop as the stronghold of socialism, 'pure' socialism. The books were kept by a man whose face was almost impossible to see because of a beard which grew up to his eyes, or better, up to his pince-nez. (It was a pince-nez period.) Errands were run by a lame eccentric called Etienne who hopped about in a long white blouse reaching down to his calves. A black cat, which had adopted the 'cité harmonieuse' as its abiding home, slept on the stacks of unsold copies of Joan of Arc. Once in a while, there was a little excitement: a band of royalists would smash a window in Péguy's shop, invectives were exchanged and walking sticks went into action in true 1898 fashion. There was quite an arsenal of walking sticks at the 'cité harmonieuse'. We are apt to forget what a prominent part was played by sticks in those days. Péguy had one which his mother-in-law had given him; he was extremely proud of this object which was finally broken in two over his back by an irate policeman, at the time of Zola's trial.

However stimulating the presence of the socialist strong-hold may have been to the Latin Quarter, the financial situation of Péguy's bookshop was disastrous. No one could be persuaded to buy 'Jeanne d'Arc'. At last, the shop was saved from complete bankruptcy by a group of men who decided to take it over. One of these men was Léon Blum, who struggled vainly, in later years, to make France into a cité harmonieuse.

Péguy, however, felt that the shop was being taken out of his hands, and in 1901 he decided to take himself and his unsold books to other premises in the rue de la Sorbonne. Etienne, the old errand boy, was dismissed because he helped himself too freely to whatever money he found in the counter, but it was very characteristic of Péguy that he did not reproach Etienne with this little failing. Etienne was also extremely reluctant when it came to working and on this score alone Péguy decided that he must be sent away. A formula had to be found which would at once inform Etienne of the bad news and spare his sensitiveness. Péguy could not think of anything. Finally, one of his friends hit upon what he considered a happy phrase. So Etienne was summoned and the following speech fell upon his ears: 'Etienne, we must part. It has been brought to our attention that you do not quit yourself of your duty with the necessary *intensity.*' And somehow, Etienne understood and left. I have mentioned this very small incident because I think it gives an idea of these people's kindness and seriousness.

Péguy's new bookstore was as austere as a monastery and a very strict discipline reigned between its walls, an almost military discipline. Indeed there always was a suggestion of the military about Péguy, and of the religious as well. And

in spite of his interest in modern politics, he was anything but a man of his time. There was a telephone in the shop, but he never touched it, he preferred to wrap himself up in his cape and cross the river rather than speak into a receiver to a friend.

His book-keeper in the rue de la Sorbonne was an old school-mate by the name of Bourgeois. Such a conscientious book-keeper as Bourgeois could never be found. He was what the French call *sérieux*. Péguy was very fond of repeating that one must be *sérieux* and Bourgeois was as serious as could be desired. At that time, Péguy had started a publishing business, the books published being written by Péguy and his friends. They came out regularly, like the issues of a magazine, and were called the Fortnightly Note-books. Need I say that they were nearly all written in an intensely serious vein. They dealt mostly with social problems and the City of the Future and, of course, letters were exchanged between the publishers and their subscribers. Bourgeois answered these letters. He even answered letters which required no answers. He answered to say that there was no answer. Financial settlements were treated with the same thoroughness. If, for instance, the sum of two hundred and seventeen francs and twenty-five centimes was owed, the pennies were paid as well as the francs, which was naturally expected, but if the sum happened to be two hundred and seventeen francs and twenty-three centimes, the twenty-three centimes were paid, thus causing astonishment and admiration, because, as is well known, the French penny is worth five centimes, and five centimes, even in 1900, was so very small a sum that it was practically never divided. It was called a *sou*, a *petit sou*, the *gros sou* being worth ten centimes. Beggars in

the street would ask for 'un petit sou, s'il vous plaît, Monsieur', adding as a rule that the good Lord would give it back to you. You couldn't decently give less than a sou, because it was impossible to buy anything with less than a sou, except one centime stamps, and the centime as a coin was almost never used, except by Bourgeois who thought that if you owed a man two centimes, the two centimes had to be paid, and that to overlook such a debt was in itself an act of injustice.

Péguy's time was divided between his publishing firm and the writing of his own books. He wrote regularly, but he never knew what he was going to write when he sat down to his sheet of white paper. The idea of making a draught of what he wanted to express was completely foreign to him. His life was more and more like a long meditation interrupted only by conversations, sometimes impassioned arguments with his friends. Nobody could be as silent as Péguy, nor could anyone talk so much. What he wrote proceeded directly from silence but must have been colored by his talks. Not a word was ever scratched out. If a word came to him, he argued, it had as much right to be written down as all its fellow-words in the book. It was there as a witness, like a pebble on the long road he travelled. Péguy considered that what he wrote had been dictated to him. When he wanted to praise a book, or a sentence in a book, he never said: 'It is good', he said: 'It is dictated.'

No book was ever brought out by the *Cahiers de la Quinzaine* without first having been read by Péguy. It is a well-known fact that almost every book we read, except the best editions of the Bible, contains misprints. Misprints are, in a way, almost inevitable nowadays, because, however careful we may seem in our own eyes, most of us are in a tearing

hurry (although where all this hurry is going to get us, I don't know). But there were no misprints in the books published by Péguy. A great French publisher, Edouard Pelletan, once said that Charles Péguy could be compared only to the sixteenth century printers, who were real printers, not amateurs. We are amateurs in many ways. We are amateurs when we write, we are amateurs when we think, we are sometimes amateurs when we wage war, we are often amateurs when we pray, because we are in a hurry, because we are not *sérieux*. Péguy was not an amateur. When he corrected a book, he did not read it, he searched for misprints, and when he said that the book had been corrected, it was corrected such as no book in France had been corrected.

While Péguy was busy laying the plans of the City of the Future, times were slowly moving and changing, even though the world was not aware that it was passing from a period to an epoch, the end of which is not yet within sight. On June 4, 1905, a German cuirassier wearing a flashy white uniform, got off a battleship and entered the city of Tangiers on the coast of Morocco. It was the Kaiser. On June 5, Charles Péguy, accompanied by his wife, went to one of the largest stores in Paris, the *Bon Marché*, and bought woolen socks, heavy underwear and other things a soldier may need who is going to the front. He did all this with his usual seriousness, prophesying that the history of his country and of the whole world was coming to a turning point. He did not fear war; he had always expected it to come and now he was ready, but there were nine more years to wait before the storm broke out, and after a few days excitement, Péguy found himself working again in a once more peaceful Paris.

The next few years of Péguy's life were marked by sad-

ness and disillusionments of all kinds. To begin with, there
was a fearful financial struggle to keep the *Cahiers* going.
Some of them proved difficult reading, even when Péguy
wrote the preface, which added considerably to the bulk of
the volume. A number of *Cahiers* were entirely filled with
Péguy's own words, bold, often indignant words in defense
of the working classes and in attacks on our modern world
which he hated. But the modern world cared little whether
Péguy hated it or not and scarcely knew his name. There
were other worries too. Péguy was strongheaded, obstinate
and very jealous of the authority he exercised over his
friends; as they grew older, however, admiration no longer
prevented them from disagreeing with him and, in Péguy's
eyes, these disagreements became acts of treason. He quarrelled with most of his friends, with Lucien Herr, with Jean-
Pierre Laurens, with Psichari, Renan's grandson who became
a Catholic, with Pierre Mille and André Spire, with Daniel
Halévy, and he quarrelled with Jacques Maritain. To us who
know the great Catholic philosopher, this seems almost incredible. Whenever an important issue was at stake, Maritain
has shown an indomitable firmness of spirit and I venture
to say that, if Péguy were to return to life in our distracted
world of 1942, he could not be prouder of any other friend
of his; but, whatever may be our reasons for admiring
Maritain, it is his kindliness and humanity which have en-
deared him to so many. I have been told, however, on best
authority, that he and Charles Péguy were reconciled in later
years. Of their quarrel I shall say nothing, except that it
seems to me to have been unduly emphasized by writers who
were not present when the events they describe actually
occurred.

One day in September 1908, Péguy had a conversation
with his friend Lotte, about his many worries, when all of a
sudden his eyes filled with tears and he said: 'I have not told
you all. I have found faith again. I am a Catholic.' This was
the outcome of a long struggle about which we know practically nothing. What went on in Péguy's soul from the time
he declared himself an atheist, around '92 or '93, to the min-
ute when he unburdened his heart to Lotte is a mystery which
will probably never be solved. Nor did this conversion mean
a simplifying of life's problems for Péguy. On the contrary.
Only from the outside do conversions appear to simplify
life's problems. A conversion does not mean that the fight
is over and that peace will necessarily reign forever. In
Péguy's case it meant quite the opposite. To begin with, there
was the fact that he had married into a family of staunch
unbelievers and that his children, two boys and a girl, were
unbaptized, nor would Madame Péguy hear of having them
baptized. And, of course, in the eyes of the Church, he and
Madame Péguy were not married. So it was impossible for
Péguy to live as a Catholic and he did not go to mass. Even
to this day, we are not sure that he ever went to communion
after his conversion; it is believed that he received the Sacrament a few weeks before he was killed, but his son Marcel
states very definitely that this fact cannot be 'historically
proved'.

What spiritual agony this must have meant to Péguy, we
can only guess, and faintly guess. He prayed incessantly as
he walked from one end of Paris to the other, or on the tops
of 'omnibuses' with his beads in his hands and tears running
down his face. We can be sure that Péguy did not pray like
an amateur; he prayed with the obstinate faith of a medieval

peasant, and yet here too were difficulties, for instance that sentence in the Lord's prayer in which we beg for forgiveness was a stumbling-block to Péguy who insisted that we do not forgive those who trespass against us. But the important thing was that he had taken the step which leads from the outer darkness of atheism to the world of Christ, and the tears that ran down his cheeks may not always have been tears of grief.

Early in 1910, what Péguy had confidentially told Lotte was to be publicly avowed in a work which will no doubt make its author's name last for centuries in Catholic France. It bore a long title which reminds one of a heavy granite lintel over an ancient doorway: 'The Mystery of the Charity of Joan of Arc.' Very few noticed the book, fewer still realized its importance. The 'Mystery' was published as a *Cahier* but most probably the subscribers did not even cut its leaves. What they wanted was Romain Rolland's clumsy books, and they tolerated Péguy because they knew that, sooner or later, a Romain Rolland would be sent to them. Critics hardly noticed the poem or had little to say about it that might please the author. True, one critic wrote that it was the greatest Catholic poem ever written since the Divine Comedy, but that critic's name was Lotte, and the article had been dictated to him by Péguy.

'The Mystery of the Charity of Joan of Arc' has much in common with the opening act of the first Joan of Arc, the socialist Joan of Arc, as that early work is sometimes called, but in the 'Mystery', the blanks have been filled and filled in such a way that Péguy at once took his place among the greatest poets of his country. The principal theme of this poem (which we might hesitate to call a play) is the awakening of Joan of Arc's vocation. Indeed nothing actually hap-

pens which could properly claim the name of action, nor does anything happen in the second and third Mysteries which followed in 1911 and 1912. On the other hand, it does not seem possible to describe this work as a philosophical poem, because philosophical poems as a rule are not without at least a suggestion of boredom or tedious abstractness which is wholly lacking in Péguy's Mysteries. Péguy shared with Dante the peculiar gift of clothing the metaphysical with humanity. He had an eye for the invisible which only the most mystical among primitives have had before him, because he was himself a great primitive and there is nothing in literature more suggestive of Dirk Bouts or Rogier van der Weyden than his vision of Mary following her son up Mount Calvary, in the passage which I have ventured to translate as 'The Passion of Our Lady'.

In trying to give, not an equivalent of some of Péguy's lines in English—that I could never do—but what I hope is a faithful rendering of his meaning, I have endeavored to preserve the great simplicity of language which marks the original. Péguy's words are words which a French child, or a French workman, or a French peasant could easily understand. In fact, God the Father, as presented by Péguy in these Mysteries, speaks somewhat like an elderly French peasant well versed in his catechism, rather than like a professor who has read Saint Thomas, as we might have dreaded. His language is at times so plain that its very plainness defies translation. Of the speeches themselves, particularly those spoken by God the Father, I can only say very little. What characterizes them, I think, is a sort of supernatural common sense and an internal rhythm, a rhythm of thought which lends them majesty and pathos. There is in them a beauty

of reasoning and a sort of medieval instinct which we seem
to have lost for thinking in terms of the universe. Charity
and intellect go hand in hand, intellect always ready to efface
itself before charity which is, after all, nothing but a superior
form of understanding. Péguy was essentially human and
anything that smacked of pedantry was abhorrent to him.
'Je suis un auteur gai', he used to say. In consequence, his
God the Father, although he is as strict a logician as a Frenchman can be, never discourages a joke, provided it is neither
rude nor unkind, nor is he averse to joking himself, for his
pre-eminent wisdom never stands in the way of his sense
of humor.

To a French reader of 1912, Péguy's style must have
caused extreme surprise. We are so used to it now that it
seems almost inevitable that such a style should have been
invented to express a certain form of religious emotion.
Péguy had a very deep-rooted belief in the force of repetition, not idle repetition for repetition's sake, as we find it in
more recent poets, not repetition of a word, or of a set of
words, because they happen to please the author's ear, but
repetition for the sake of clearness, repetition, also, to per-
suade and to convince. Péguy repeats himself, but he repeats
himself as Bach does, that is, each repetition is enriched with
a new meaning and adds to what has already been said. Indeed, music is almost irresistibly suggested by Péguy's mono-
logues, not so much because of the fullness and beauty of
their sound as by an impression of building which music also
conveys, an impression of walls and towers being raised and
arches vaulting over great heights.

The second Mystery came out in October 1911 under the
title of 'The Porch of the Mystery of the Second Virtue,' the

second virtue being, of course, the theological virtue of hope. Here, Péguy's faith seemed to have reached its highest point. There was still anxious questioning in the first Mystery, but now, under the guidance of hope, he had rediscovered the 'way of childhood'. Less than half a year after that, the third Mystery appeared. It was called 'The Mystery of the Holy Innocents' and dealt principally with what might be termed the perfection of confidence in God.

Almost complete silence greeted these magnificent poems. Criticisms had been made and, in one famous instance, doubts had been expressed as to the authenticity of Péguy's Catholicism when the first Mystery was published, but now, remembering the poet's furious retorts in 1910, the professional critics held their peace. The public hardly suspected that Péguy existed, and smart people who knew about books read Anatole France and d'Annunzio.

Nevertheless, Péguy kept on. His forebodings of an early death were more and more frequent and yet, he said, he must not die. There was still a tremendous number of things to be written about, Paradise for instance. He wanted to write a poem on Paradise, but not like Dante's, he explained. Péguy's ambition was to fill his Paradise with all the things he considered worth saving, Notre Dame of Paris and Notre Dame of Chartres among others, to say nothing of countless villages of France and all the tools which hard-working humanity has used since the beginning. No doubt he would also have found room for one or two of those chairs which his mother mended so well. But he did not have time to indulge very much longer in what has been called his delirium of enumeration. His last long poem, 'Eve', was published in December 1913. Its main theme is the salvation of the human race and in

many respects it is a very great piece of work, but I do not think many people have read it in its entirety at one or even two sittings, not that its length might deter a serious reader, but repetitions occur with an almost maddening frequency and only slight variations of meaning. I have often had the book in hand and have invariably closed it with mixed feelings of admiration and alarm. It has the hypnotic force of an incantation. *'Ah, les mots, mon vieux, les mots!'* Péguy used to say to his friends. No one ever loved the beauty of words more than he did, and here we see him intoxicated with his own words. His often quoted lines about death on the battlefield lay buried in this gigantic poem for several years before they were discovered and first applied to him; they did much for his present fame.

Péguy's conversion did not draw him away from humanity, as so frequently happens. To begin with, he did not want to be called a convert. He had never really changed. To use the old Greek phrase, he had become what he was, he had never ceased to belong to the old France of his peasant ancestors, and their faith was his faith. Like Joan of Arc herself, he could recite (almost) Our Father, and Hail Mary, and the Creed, and the long litanies with their heavenly repetitions. But the dream of a world revolution was not forgotten: it was merely transferred to a higher plane. Péguy knew very well that the Church is, in its essence, revolutionary, that one of its many tasks on earth is to overthrow the old pagan order, still so very firmly established in this world. When Saint Francis preached on the holiness of poverty, he was a far greater revolutionist than Lenin, but he had no blood on his hands except the blood of the stigmata. Charles Péguy never gave up the hope of a blessed revolution whereby all

bad men would be turned into good men, and poverty would
be honored, and peace prevail. These dreams may seem
somewhat pathetic to us, in 1942, but we must not forget that
man has always believed in them, that they are at the base
of the teachings of the prophets, that they shine through the
pages of the New Testament, and that when they seem very
remote or even ridiculous, it merely means that our conscience is being obscured by some shocking crisis like the
one we are going through now.

One year before he was killed, Péguy's faith was put to a
test. One of his sons fell desperately ill with typhoid fever
and there seemed to be little hope of saving him. Péguy did
what a medieval Frenchman would have done, because he
was a medieval Frenchman, he spoke earnestly to Our Lady
about his unbaptized children, one of whom was in danger
of death. He could not look after them. 'I have enormous re-
sponsibilities,' he explained to the Queen of Heaven. 'You
must do something for my children. I place them in your
lap, I give them to you, and now I am going away before
you can give them back to me.'

The sick child recovered. Naturally, said Péguy who
showed no surprise (he knew how to ask).* However, he
had promised Our Lady of Chartres to make a pilgrimage
to her church if his child was saved, but he was not in a
hurry to redeem his promise; he was never in a hurry about
anything. Several months went by, then he put on his heavy
shoes, took his stick and started out on foot in the direction
of Chartres. There are seventy-two kilometers between Paris
and Chartres and it took Péguy three days to cover that

---

* Later his children were baptized. His wife became a Catholic after his death.

distance. He left us an account of his pilgrimage in a poem
which, by a caprice of fate, brought him something like
recognition a few months before he died.

When the war broke out, Péguy was forty-one and should
normally have been in the reserve, but to a man of his type,
this was simply unacceptable. Early in August, he left for the
front with his regiment, having been given the rank of lieu-
tenant. There was no mistake about it this time: he was living, at last, in an epoch. All during the harrowing month of
August, the German armies swept through Northern France
until they were stopped, in the first week of September, along
the river Marne. Péguy's regiment was in the neighborhood
of Senlis. On the third of September, they were quartered
for a few hours in a deserted convent. Péguy spent that night
decorating the altar of Our Lady with flowers which he had
picked. On the fourth, he and his men moved on in the direction of Meaux. On the fifth, in the early part of the after-
noon, they were in the neighborhood of Villeroy with shells
bursting all around them. The men ran a few yards forward,
then stopped and threw themselves on the ground to shoot
at the already retreating Germans. But Péguy did not lie
down. There he stood in his red and blue uniform, a living
target in the blazing sun, telling his men to shoot at will,
then running ahead of them to lead them on. They all shouted
to him to lie down, but he, with an oath, told them to keep
on shooting. The last thing he probably saw was the German
line wavering and falling back. A bullet struck him in the
forehead and he fell with a groan as his men ran to victory.
When they looked for his body after the battle was over, they
had some trouble in identifying it, but a friend of his finally
succeeded in doing so: he found a coin in one of the dead

man's pockets, a one *centime* piece, one of Bourgeois'
centimes.

Blessed are those who died in great battles,
Stretched out on the ground in the face of God,
Blessed are those who died in a just war,
Blessed is the wheat that is ripe and the wheat that is gathered
     in sheaves.

    Thus wrote Péguy, in 1913, under the dictation of his
prophetic soul.

                                                  Julian Green.

VERITES FONDAMENTALES

BASIC VERITIES

LES HONNETES GENS

Nous sommes ici des catholiques qui ne trichent pas; des protestants qui ne trichent pas; des juifs qui ne trichent pas; des libres penseurs qui ne trichent pas. C'est pour ça que nous sommes si peu de catholiques; si peu de protestants; si peu de juifs; si peu de libres penseurs. Et en tout si peu de monde. Et nous avons contre nous les catholiques qui trichent; les protestants qui trichent; les juifs qui trichent; les libres penseurs qui trichent. — Et ça fait beaucoup de monde. Outre que tous les tricheurs ont une sûreté pour se reconnaître entre eux et pour s'appuyer; une sûreté infaillible; une sûreté invincible; pour se soutenir; une sûreté inexpiable. Une sûreté d'instinct, une sûreté de race, le seul instinct qu'ils aient, qui n'est comparable qu'à la sûreté profonde avec laquelle les médiocres reconnaissent et appuient les médiocres. Mais au fond n'est-ce pas la même? Et ne sont-ils pas les mêmes? Si seulement nous les honnêtes gens nous étions fidèles à l'honnêteté comme la médiocrité est fidèle à la médiocrité.

THE HONEST PEOPLE

HERE, WE ARE CATHOLICS who don't cheat; protestants who don't cheat; Jews who don't cheat; freethinkers who don't cheat. That is why we are so few catholics; so few protestants; so few Jews; so few freethinkers. And in all, so few of us. And against us we have the catholics who cheat; the protestants who cheat; the Jews who cheat; the free-thinkers who cheat.—And that makes a lot of people. Besides this, all the cheats have a sureness in recognizing and stand-ing by one another; an infallible sureness; an invincible sureness; to support each other; an unatonable sureness. An instinctive sureness, a sureness pertaining to the race, the only instinct which they possess, comparable alone to the deep sureness with which the mediocre know and support the mediocre. But at bottom is it not the same? And are they not the same? If only we honest people were faithful to honesty as mediocrity is faithful to mediocrity.

MALHEUR AUX TIEDES. Honte au honteux. Malheur et honte
à celui qui a honte. Il ne s'agit point tant ici encore de croire
ou de ne pas croire. — Honte à celui qui renierait son Dieu
pour ne point faire sourire les gens d'esprit. Honte à celui qui
renierait sa foi pour ne pas donner dans le ridicule, pour ne
point prêter à sourire, pour ne point passer pour un imbécile.
Il s'agit ici de l'homme qui ne s'occupe point de savoir s'il
croit ou s'il ne croit pas. — Il s'agit de l'homme qui vendrait
son Dieu pour ne pas être ridicule. — Il s'agit de l'homme, du
malheureux apeuré, qui regarde de tous les côtés, qui lance
timoré des regards circonvoisins pour être bien sûr que quelqu'un de l'honorable assistance n'a point souri de lui, de sa
foi, de son Dieu. C'est l'homme qui lance tout autour de lui
des regards préventifs. Sur la société. Des regards de con-
nivence. C'est l'homme qui tremble. C'est l'homme dont le
regard demande pardon d'avance pour Dieu; dans les salons.

QUI NE GUEULE PAS la vérité, quand il sait la vérité, se fait
le complice des menteurs et des faussaires.

IL FAUT TOUJOURS dire ce que l'on voit. Surtout il faut
toujours, ce qui est plus difficile, voir ce que l'on voit.

UN MOT N'EST PAS le même dans un écrivain et dans un
autre. L'un se l'arrache du ventre. L'autre le tire de la poche
de son pardessus.

WOE TO THE LUKEWARM. Shame on him who is ashamed. Woe to and shame on him who is ashamed. The question here is not so much to believe or not to believe.—Shame on the man who would deny his God to avoid raising a smile among the witty. Shame on the man who would deny his faith to avoid ridicule, to avoid being laughed at, to avoid being branded a fool. The question here concerns the man who does not trouble to find out whether he believes or does not believe.— The question concerns the man who would sell his God to avoid being ridiculous.—The question concerns the man, the wretched craven, who looks all about him, who casts timid glances around him, to be quite sure that no one in the honorable company has smiled at him, at his faith, at his God. This is the man who casts precautionary glances all around him. On society. Glances of connivance. This is the man who trembles. This is the man whose look, beforehand, begs pardon for God; in drawing rooms.

HE WHO DOES NOT BELLOW the truth when he knows the truth makes himself the accomplice of liars and forgers.

ONE MUST ALWAYS TELL what one sees. Above all, which is more difficult, one must always see what one sees.

A WORD IS NOT the same with one writer as with another. One tears it from his guts. The other pulls it out of his overcoat pocket.

LA RECHERCHE DE LA VERITE

J E CROIS que l'on trouverait aisément dans l'histoire du
monde un très grand nombre d'exemples de personnes
qui apercevant soudain la vérité, la saisissant, ou l'ayant
cherchée l'ayant trouvée, rompent délibérément avec leurs
intérêts, sacrifient leurs intérêts, rompent délibérément avec
leurs amitiés politiques et même avec leurs amitiés senti-
mentales. Je ne crois pas que l'on trouve beaucoup d'exemples
d'hommes qui ayant accompli ce premier sacrifice, et s'apercevant ensuite, comme il arrive communément, que leurs
nouveaux amis ne valent pas mieux que les anciens, que
leurs deuxièmes amis ne valent pas mieux que les premiers,
aient eu le deuxième courage de sacrifier aussi délibérément leurs deuxièmes intérêts, leurs deuxièmes amitiés.
Malheur à l'homme seul, et ce qu'ils redoutent le plus dans
la création, c'est la solitude. Ils veulent bien, pour la vérité,
se brouiller avec une moitié du monde. D'autant qu'en se
brouillant ainsi avec une moitié du monde, non sans un peu
de retentissement, ils se font généralement des partisans de
l'autre moitié du monde, qui ne demande pas mieux que
d'être antagoniste à la première. Mais si, pour l'amour de
cette même vérité, ils vont se mettre sottement à rompre avec
cette deuxième moitié, qui sera leurs partisans? —

THE SEARCH FOR TRUTH

I BELIEVE that in the history of the world one could easily find a very great number of examples of persons who, suddenly perceiving the truth, seize it. Or, having sought and found it, deliberately break with their interests, sacrifice their interests, break deliberately with their political friendships and even with their sentimental friendships. I do not believe that one finds many examples of men who, having accomplished this first sacrifice, have had the second courage to sacrifice their second interests, their second friendships. For it commonly happens that they find their new friends are worth no more than the old ones, that their second friends are worth no more than the first. *Woe to the lonely man,* and what they fear most is solitude. They are most willing, for the sake of the truth, to fall out with half of the world. All the more so when, by thus falling out with half of the world—not without a little repercussion—they usually make partisans among the second half of the world; partisans who ask nothing better than to be the antagonists of the first half. But if, for the love of this same truth, they foolishly go about breaking with this second half, who will become their partisans?—

Un homme courageux, et il n'y en a déjà pas beaucoup, rompt pour la vérité avec ses amis et ses intérêts; ainsi se forme un nouveau parti, qui est originairement et censément le parti de la justice et de la vérité, qui en moins de rien devient absolument identique aux autres partis; un parti comme les autres, comme tous les autres; aussi vulgaire; aussi grossier; aussi injuste; aussi faux; alors, à cette deuxième fois, il faudrait un homme surcourageux pour opérer une deuxième rupture: il n'y en a pour ainsi dire plus. —

Et pourtant il faut que la vie de l'honnête homme soit une apostasie et une renégation perpétuelle, il faut que l'honnête homme soit un perpétuel renégat, il faut que la vie de l'honnête homme soit une infidélité perpétuelle. Car l'homme qui veut demeurer fidèle à la vérité doit se faire incessamment infidèle à toutes les incessantes, successives, infatigables renaissantes erreurs. Et l'homme qui veut demeurer fidèle à la justice doit se faire incessamment infidèle aux injustices inépuisablement triomphantes.

L'HUMANITE DEPASSERA les premiers dirigeables comme elle a dépassé les premières locomotives. Elle dépassera M. Santos-Dumont comme elle a dépassé Stephenson. Après la té-léphotographie elle inventera tout le temps des graphies et des scopies et des phonies, qui ne seront pas moins *télé* les unes que les autres, et l'on pourra faire le tour de la terre en moins de rien. Mais ce ne sera jamais que la terre temporelle. Et même entrer dedans et la transpercer d'outre en outre comme je fais cette boule de glaise. Mais ce ne sera jamais que la terre charnelle. Et on ne voit pas que nul homme jamais, ni aucune humanité, en un certain sens, qui est le bon, puisse intelligemment se vanter d'avoir dépassé Platon. Je vais plus

A brave man—and so far, there are not many—for the sake of the truth breaks with his friends and his interests. Thus a new party is formed, originally and supposedly the party of justice and truth, which in less than no time becomes absolutely identical with the other parties. A party like the others; like all the others; as vulgar; as gross; as unjust; as false. Then for this second time, a superbrave man would have to be found to make a second break: but of these, there are hardly any left.—

And yet, the life of an honest man must be an apostasy and a perpetual desertion. The honest man must be a perpetual renegade, the life of an honest man must be a perpetual infidelity. For the man who wishes to remain faithful to truth must make himself continually unfaithful to all the continual, successive, indefatigable renascent errors. And the man who wishes to remain faithful to justice must make himself continually unfaithful to inexhaustibly triumphant injustices.

HUMANITY WILL SURPASS the first dirigibles as it has surpassed the first locomotives. It will surpass M. Santos-Dumont as it has surpassed Stephenson. After telephotography it will continually invent graphies and scopes and phones, all of which will be *tele* and one will be able to go around the earth in less than no time. But it will always only be the temporal earth. And it will even be possible to burrow inside the earth and pierce it through and through as I do this ball of clay. But it will always only be the carnal earth. And it cannot be imagined that any man ever, nor any humanity, in a certain sense—which is the right sense—can ever intelligently boast of having surpassed Plato. I will go further. I add that a

loin. J'ajoute qu'un homme cultivé, vraiment cultivé, ne comprend pas, ne peut pas même imaginer ce que cela pourrait bien vouloir dire que de prétendre avoir dépassé Platon.

UNE GRANDE PHILOSOPHIE n'est pas celle qui prononce des jugements définitifs, qui installe une vérité définitive. C'est celle qui introduit une inquiétude, qui ouvre un ébranlement. —
Une grande philosophie n'est pas celle qui n'est jamais battue. Mais une petite philosophie est toujours celle qui ne se bat pas. — Une grande philosophie n'est pas une philosophie sans reproche, c'est une philosophie sans peur.

LE GENIE n'est point du talent porté à un très haut degré, ni même à sa limite, mais il est d'un autre ordre que le talent.

C'EST LE PROPRE du génie que de procéder par les idées les plus simples.

L'AMOUR EST PLUS RARE que le génie même. — Et l'amitié est plus rare que l'amour.

LA PIRE DES PARTIALITES est de se refuser, la pire ignorance est de n'agir pas, le mensonge le pire est de se dérober.

TOUT PERE sur qui son fils lève la main est coupable: d'avoir fait un fils qui levât la main sur lui.

QUAND UN HOMME SE MEURT, il ne meurt pas seulement de la maladie qu'il a. Il meurt de toute sa vie.

cultured man, a really cultured man, cannot even imagine the meaning of a claim to have surpassed Plato.

A GREAT PHILOSOPHY is not that which passes final judgments, which takes a seat in final truth. It is that which introduces uneasiness, which opens the door to commotion.—
A great philosophy is not that which is never defeated. But a small philosophy is always that which does not fight.—A great philosophy is not a philosophy without reproach, it is a philosophy without fear.

GENIUS IS NOT TALENT brought to a very high degree, nor even to its limit, but it is of another order than talent.

IT IS IN THE INNATE CHARACTER of genius to proceed by the simplest ideas.

LOVE IS RARER than genius itself.—And friendship is rarer than love.

THE WORST OF PARTIALITIES is to withhold oneself, the worst ignorance is not to act, the worst lie is to steal away.

ANY FATHER whose son strikes him is guilty: of having conceived a son capable of striking him.

WHEN A MAN LIES DYING, he does not die from disease alone. He dies from his whole life.

MISERE ET PAUVRETE

ON CONFOND presque toujours la misère avec la pauvreté; cette confusion vient de ce que la misère et la pauvreté sont voisines; elles sont voisines sans doute, mais situées de part et d'autre d'une limite. — Tout est misère en deçà, misère du doute ou misère de la certitude misérable; la première zone au delà est celle de la pauvreté; puis s'étagent les zones successives des richesses.

Beaucoup de problèmes économiques, moraux ou sociaux, politiques même seraient préalablement éclairés si l'on y introduisait, ou plutôt si l'on y reconnaissait comme due la considération de cette limite. —

La misère est tout le domaine en deçà de cette limite; la pauvreté commence au delà et finit tôt; ainsi la misère et la pauvreté sont voisines; elles sont plus voisines en quantité, que certaines richesses ne le sont de la pauvreté; si on évalue selon la quantité seule, un riche est beaucoup plus éloigné d'un pauvre qu'un pauvre n'est éloigné d'un miséreux; mais entre la misère et la pauvreté intervient une limite; et le pauvre est séparé du miséreux par un écart de qualité, de nature. —

DESTITUTION AND POVERTY

DESTITUTION IS ALMOST ALWAYS CONFUSED with poverty; this mistake comes from the fact that destitution and poverty are neighbors. No doubt they are neighbors, but situated on either side of a boundary.—All is misery within the boundary; misery of uncertainty or misery of certain destitution. The first zone beyond the boundary is that of poverty. After which rise, tier upon tier, the successive zones of riches.

Many economic, moral, social, or even political problems could be clarified in advance if the consideration of this boundary were introduced—or rather, if this consideration were recognized as a duty.—

Destitution is the entire domain within this boundary. Poverty begins beyond it and ends early. Thus destitution and poverty are neighbors. They are closer neighbors in quantity than certain riches are neighbors of poverty. If one evaluates according to quantity alone, a rich man is much farther removed from a poor man than a poor man is removed from a destitute man. But between destitution and poverty a boundary arises. And the poor man is separated from the destitute man by a difference of quality, of nature.—

Comme il y a entre les situations où gisent les miséreux
et la situation où les pauvres vivent une différence de qualité,
il y a ainsi entre les devoirs qui intéressent les miséreux
et les devoirs qui intéressent les pauvres une différence de
qualité; arracher les miséreux à la misère est un devoir antérieur, antécédent; aussi longtemps que les miséreux ne
sont pas retirés de la misère, les problèmes de la cité ne se
posent pas; retirer de la misère les miséreux, sans aucune
exception, constitue le devoir social avant l'accomplissement
duquel on ne peut pas même examiner quel est le premier
devoir social. —

Je demande pardon d'insister autant sur la misère; c'est un
sujet ingrat; une conspiration générale du silence nous laisserait croire que la misère n'existe pas. —

Nous ne pouvons pas, ce serait commode, mais nous ne
pouvons pas croire qu'il n'y a pas de misère parce que nous
ne la regardons pas; elle est quand même, et nous regarde.
Nous ne pouvons pas invoquer les sentiments de la solidarité
pour demander à la misère de nous laisser la paix; nous
sommes forcés d'aller jusqu'aux sentiments de la charité;
mais il suffit de la solidarité pour que la misère puisse nous
requérir. —

Le devoir d'arracher les misérables à la misère et le devoir
de répartir également les biens ne sont pas du même ordre:
le premier est un devoir d'urgence; le deuxième est un
devoir de convenance; non seulement les trois termes de la
devise républicaine, liberté, égalité, fraternité, ne sont pas
sur le même plan, mais les deux derniers eux-mêmes, qui
sont plus approchés entre eux qu'ils ne sont tous deux proches
du premier, présentent plusieurs différences notables; par
la fraternité nous sommes tenus d'arracher à la misère nos

Just as there is a difference of quality between the conditions in which the destitute lie and those in which the poor live, so there is a difference of quality in the duties which concern the destitute and in those which concern the poor. To tear the destitute from destitution is a prior and preliminary duty. So long as the destitute are not removed from their destitution, the problems of the city do not present themselves. To remove the destitute, without a single exception, from destitution constitutes the social duty before the accomplishment of which one cannot even examine what the first social duty is to be.—

I apologize for laying so much stress on destitution. It is an unpleasant subject. A general conspiracy of silence would lead us to believe that destitution does not exist.—

We cannot—it would be convenient—but we cannot believe that there is no destitution simply because we do not look at it. It is there, just the same, and looks at us. We cannot invoke sentiments of solidarity in order to ask destitution to leave us in peace. For that we are obliged to go as far as sentiments of charity. But for destitution to summon us, solidarity is sufficient.—

The duty of tearing the destitute from destitution and the duty of distributing goods equitably are not of the same order. The first is an urgent duty, the second is a duty of convenience. Not only are the three terms of the republican device, Liberty, Equality, Fraternity not on the same plane, but the last two, which are nearer to each other than both are near the first, present several notable differences. Fraternity obliges us to tear our fellow-men from destitution. That is a preliminary duty. Contrarily, equality is a far less pressing duty. Whereas it is intensely pressing and alarming to know

frères les hommes; c'est un devoir préalable; au contraire le
devoir d'égalité est un devoir beaucoup moins pressant;
autant il est passionnant, inquiétant de savoir qu'il y a encore
des hommes dans la misère, autant il m'est égal de savoir
si, hors de la misère, les hommes ont des morceaux plus ou
moins grands de fortune; je ne puis parvenir à me passionner
pour la question célèbre de savoir à qui reviendra, dans la
cité future, les bouteilles de champagne, les chevaux rares,
les châteaux de la vallée de la Loire; j'espère qu'on s'ar-
rangera toujours; pourvu qu'il y ait vraiment une cité, c'est-
à-dire pourvu qu'il n'y ait aucun homme qui soit banni de
la cité, tenu en exil dans la misère économique, tenu dans
l'exil économique, peu m'importe que tel ou tel ait telle ou
telle situation; de bien autres problèmes solliciteront sans
doute l'attention des citoyens; au contraire il suffit qu'un seul
homme soit tenu sciemment, ou, ce qui revient au même,
sciemment laissé dans la misère pour que le pacte civique
tout entier soit nul; aussi longtemps qu'il y a un homme
dehors, la porte qui lui est fermée au nez ferme une cité
d'injustice et de haine.

Le problème de la misère n'est pas sur le même plan, n'est
pas du même ordre que le problème de l'inégalité. Ici encore
les anciennes préoccupations, les préoccupations tradition-
nelles, instinctives de l'humanité se trouvent à l'analyse beaucoup plus profondes, beaucoup plus justifiées, beaucoup plus
vraies que les récentes, et presque toujours factices, manifestations de la démocratie; sauver les misérables est un des
soucis les plus anciens de la noble humanité, persistant à
travers toutes les civilisations; d'âge en âge la fraternité,
qu'elle revête la forme de la charité ou la forme de la solidarité; qu'elle s'exerce envers l'hôte au nom de Zeus hospitalier,

that there are men still in want, the knowledge that, outside
of destitution, men possess more or less large slices of riches
does not worry me. I cannot profess much interest in the
famous question of knowing to whom bottles of champagne,
blooded horses, castles in the Loire valley, will belong in
the city of the future. I hope, that this will be settled somehow. But I really don't care if so and so has such and such a
position, as long as there will really be a city from which no
man can be banished, or held in exile by economic destitution. Doubtless many other problems will engross the attention of citizens. But to nullify the civic pact it would be
sufficient that a single man be wittingly held—or what comes
to the same—be wittingly left in destitution. As long as one
man remains outside, the door slammed in his face closes
a city of injustice and hatred.

The problem of destitution is not on the same plane, or of
the same order as the problem of inequality. Here again, the
old, traditional preoccupations, instinctive to humanity, are
found, when analyzed, to be much deeper, far better justified,
far more real than the recent and almost always artificial
manifestations of democracy. To save the destitute is one of
the oldest cares of noble humanity, persisting throughout all
civilisations. From age to age, fraternity, whether it puts on
the guise of charity or the guise of solidarity; whether it is
practised towards a guest in the name of Zeus Hospitable;
whether it welcomes the poor as an image of Jesus Christ or
whether it establishes a minimum wage for workmen; whether
it invests the citizen of the world, introducing him by baptism
into the universal communion; or whether by the improve-
ment of economic conditions it introduces him into the
international city, this fraternity is a living, deep-rooted,

qu'elle accueille le misérable comme une figure de Jésus-Christ, ou qu'elle fasse établir pour des ouvriers un minimum de salaire; qu'elle investisse le citoyen du monde, que par le baptême elle introduise à la communion universelle, ou que par le relèvement économique elle introduise dans la cité internationale, cette fraternité est un sentiment vivace, impérissable, humain; c'est un vieux sentiment, qui se maintient de forme en forme à travers les transformations, qui se lègue et se transmet de générations en générations, de culture en culture, qui de longtemps antérieur aux civilisations antiques s'est maintenu dans la civilisation chrétienne et demeure et sans doute s'épanouira dans la civilisation moderne; c'est un des meilleurs parmi les bons sentiments; c'est un sentiment à la fois profondément conservateur et profondément révolutionnaire; c'est un sentiment simple; c'est un des principaux parmi les sentiments qui ont fait l'humanité, qui l'ont maintenue, qui sans doute l'affranchiront; c'est un grand sentiment, de grande fonction, de grande histoire, et de grand avenir; c'est un grand et noble sentiment, vieux comme le monde, qui a fait le monde.

A côté de ce grand sentiment le sentiment de l'égalité paraîtra petit; moins simple aussi; quand tout homme est pourvu du nécessaire, du vrai nécessaire, du pain et du livre, que nous importe la répartition du luxe; que nous importe, en vérité, l'attribution des automobiles à deux cent cinquante chevaux, s'il y en a; il faut que les sentiments de la fraternité soient formidables pour avoir tenu en échec depuis le commencement de l'humanité, depuis l'évolution de l'animalité, tous les sentiments de la guerre, de la barbarie et de la haine, et pour avoir gagné sur eux; au contraire le sentiment de l'égalité n'est pas un vieux sentiment, un sentiment perpétuel,

imperishable human sentiment. It is an old sentiment which, maintained from form to form throughout transformations, is bequeathed and transmitted from generation to generation, from culture to culture. By far in advance of the civilisations of antiquity, it has been maintained in the Christian civilisation and remains and will doubtless flourish in modern civilisation. It is one of the best among good sentiments. It is a sentiment at once deeply conservative and deeply revolutionary. It is a simple sentiment. It is one of the principal among the sentiments which have made humanity, which have maintained it, which will doubtless free it. It is a great sentiment, one of great moment, of great history, of great future. It is a great and noble sentiment, old as the world and which has made the world.

Compared with this great sentiment, the sentiment of equality will appear small. Also, less simple. When all men are provided with the necessities, the real necessities, with bread and books, what do we care about the distribution of luxury? Indeed, what do we care about the attribution of two hundred and fifty horse power automobiles, if there be such things? Sentiments of fraternity must be formidable to have held in check, since the beginnings of humanity, since the evolution of animality, all the sentiments of war, of barbarity, of hatred, and to have won over them. On the other hand, the sentiment of equality is not an old sentiment, a perpetual sentiment, a universal sentiment of first magnitude. At determined periods it appears in the history of humanity as a peculiar phenomenon, as a manifestation of the democratic spirit. In a certain sense, sentiments of fraternity have always animated great men and great peoples, animated them, disquieted them, for preoccupation about destitution never goes

un sentiment universel, de toute grandeur; il apparaît dans l'histoire de l'humanité en des temps déterminés, comme un phénomène particulier, comme une manifestation de l'esprit démocratique; ce sont toujours, en quelque sens, les sentiments de la fraternité qui ont animé les grands hommes et les grands peuples, animé, inquiété, car la préoccupation de la misère ne va jamais sans une amertume, une inquiétude. Au contraire le sentiment de l'égalité n'a inspiré que des révolutions particulières contestables; il a opéré cette révolution anglaise, qui légua au monde moderne une Angleterre si nationaliste, impérialiste; il a opéré cette révolution américaine, qui instaura une république si impérialiste, et capitaliste; il n'a pas institué l'humanité; il n'a pas préparé la cité; il n'a instauré que des gouvernements démocratiques. C'est un sentiment composé, mêlé, souvent impur, où la vanité, l'envie, la cupidité contribuent. La fraternité inquiète, émeut, passionne les âmes profondes, sérieuses, laborieuses, modestes. L'égalité n'atteint souvent que les hommes de théâtre et de représentation, et les hommes de gouvernement; ou encore les sentiments de l'égalité sont des sentiments fabriqués, obtenus par des constructions formelles, des sentiments livresques, scolaires; quand les passions violentes, profondes et larges, humaines et populaires, s'émeuvent pour l'égalité, comme au commencement de la Révolution française, presque toujours c'est que l'égalité formelle recouvre pour sa plus grande part des réalités libertaires ou de fraternité. C'est un fait que, sauf de rares exceptions, les hommes qui ont introduit dans la politique les préoccupations d'égalité n'étaient pas, n'avaient pas été des misérables; c'étaient des petits bourgeois ou des pauvres, des notaires, des avocats, des procureurs, des hommes qui n'avaient pas reçu l'investiture indélébile de la misère.

without bitterness, disquietude. The sentiment of equality, on the other hand, has never inspired anything but questionable, particular revolutions. It brought about that English revolution which bequeathed to the modern world such a nationalistic, imperialistic England. It brought about that American revolution which established such an imperialistic and capitalistic republic. It has not inaugurated humanity. It has not prepared the city. It has only inaugurated democratic governments. It is a composite, mixed, often impure sentiment to which vanity, envy and cupidity contribute. Fraternity disquiets, moves, passionately interests deep, serious-minded, hard-working, modest souls. Equality often reaches only men loving the limelight, men loving publicity, and men of government. Or again, sentiments of equality are artificial sentiments, sentiments obtained by formal construction; bookish, scholastic sentiments. When violent passions, deep and broad, human and popular are roused on behalf of equality, as happened at the beginning of the French Revolution, it is almost always because formal equality coincides with realities of liberty and fraternity. It is a fact that, save for rare exceptions, the men who introduced preoccupations of equality into politics were not, had not been, destitute. They were middle-class men or poor men, notaries, lawyers, attorneys, men who had not received the indelible investiture of destitution.

Le vrai misérable, quand une fois il a réussi à s'évader de sa misère, en général ne demande pas son reste; les vrais misérables, une fois retirés, sont si contents d'être réchappés que, sauf de rares exceptions, ils sont contents pour le restant de leur vie; volontiers pauvres, ils sont si heureux d'avoir acquis la certitude que ce bonheur les contente; la contemplation de ce bonheur les alimente; optimistes, satisfaits, désormais soumis, doux, conservateurs, ils aiment cette résidence de quiétude; ils ne demandent pas une égalisation des richesses, parce qu'ils sentent ou parce qu'ils savent que cette égalisation n'irait pas sans de nouvelles aventures, qu'elle rouvrirait l'ère des incertitudes, qu'elle donnerait ou laisserait place au recommencement du risque; ils peuvent ainsi redouter cette égalisation comme un recommencement de la misère; ils n'en sont guère partisans; ils aiment la conservation politique et sociale, parce qu'ils aiment la conservation de la certitude; les partis de conservation n'ont pas de plus nombreux contingent, de plus compact, et solide, que celui des pauvres évadés de la misère, assurés contre la misère; anciens misérables ils ont conservé de la misère une mémoire si redoutée que ce qu'ils redoutent le plus c'est le risque. Les conservateurs modestes non réactionnaires sont les conservateurs les plus conservateurs. Ils n'ont pas du tout la passion de l'égalité. Ils ne sont pas du tout des révoltés. Ils ignorent trop souvent, ou désapprennent, les sentiments de la fraternité.

Quelques misérables au contraire ont gardé de leur misère un souvenir si anxieux qu'ils ne peuvent se tenir dans ces régions de la pauvreté, quantitativement, géographiquement voisines de la misère; ils fuient en hauteur dans les régions économiques les plus éloignées de la misère; ils deviennent

The really destitute man, once he has succeeded in escaping destitution, as a rule runs away without asking for his change. The really destitute people, having once escaped from destitution, are so happy to have escaped, that, save for rare exceptions, they are happy for the rest of their lives. Willingly poor, they are so happy to have acquired security that they are content with this happiness. The contemplation of this happiness feeds them. Optimistic, satisfied, henceforth submissive, gentle, conservative, they love this peaceful dwelling. They do not ask for equalization of wealth because they feel, or because they know, that this equalization would not go without new adventures, that it would reopen the era of uncertainties, that it would give, or leave room for the recurrence of risk. So they can fear this equalization as a recurrence of destitution. They are hardly partisans of equalization. They love political and social conservatism, because they love the conservation of security. The conservative parties have no more numerous, compact and solid contingents, than those of the poor escaped from destitution, assured against destitution. Once destitute, they have preserved such a fearful memory of destitution that what they fear most is risk. Modest, non-reactionary conservatives are the most conservative of conservatives. They do not in the least possess a passion for equality. They are not in the least rebellious. They too often ignore or unlearn the sentiments of fraternity.

On the contrary, a few among the destitute have retained such an anxious memory of their destitution that they cannot remain in those regions of poverty which are quantitatively and geographically near to destitution. They flee upwards to regions economically farthest removed from destitution. They become immensely rich, far less from cupidity for

immensément riches, beaucoup moins par cupidité des richesses que par effroi de la misère ancienne; ces malheureux
ne peuvent retrouver le repos, la paix de l'âme, que dans des
situations économiques si éloignées de leur situation première que le voyage de retour paraisse impossible à jamais;
ainsi apparaissent des ambitieux singuliers, singulièrement
formidables, ambitieux de gouvernement chez qui la passion
du gouvernement n'est pas la première, ambitieux de banque,
de commerce, d'industrie chez qui la passion du gouvernement financier, commercial, industriel, chez qui la passion
du travail, chez qui la passion d'amasser n'est pas la première; ambitieux dont les temps de grandes inventions mé-
caniques, de grandes aventures industrielles présenteraient
beaucoup d'exemples; ambitieux dont les avènements de
rois américains présenteraient des exemples particulièrement
nombreux; ambitieux dont les campagnes économiques étaient,
elles aussi, des fuites en avant. —

Telle est en effet la prolongation de la marque de la misère:
ceux qui échappent à la misère n'échappent pas à la mémoire
de leur misère; ou par continuation, ou par un effet de réac-
tion, toute leur vie ultérieure en est qualifiée; les uns, de
beaucoup les plus nombreux, se taisent dans la conservation
de la pauvreté; ils ne sont pas révolutionnaires; ils ne sont
pas égalitaires; ils demeurent au-dessous de l'égalité; les
autres, quelques-uns, ne sont révolutionnaires que pour soi;
ils ne sont pas égalitaires non plus; ils s'enfuient au-dessus
de l'égalité. Ce sont là deux démarches contraires, mais
elles ont la même cause: les uns fuient la mémoire du
risque dans l'assurance de la pauvreté; les autres fuient la
mémoire de la gêne dans l'abondance des richesses. On comp-
terait que l'immense majorité des anciens miséreux se ré-

riches than from the fear of their former destitution. These unfortunates cannot find rest or peace of mind except in conditions economically so far removed from their first condition as to make a return journey to it appear for ever impossible. Thus it is that singularly ambitious men appear, singularly formidable ones, ambitious for government, but in whom the passion for government is not the leading passion; men ambitious for banking, for commerce, for industry, in whom the passion for work, in whom the passion for accumulation is not the leading passion; ambitious men of whom times of great mechanical invention, of great industrial ventures could present many examples; ambitious men of whom the rise of American industrial barons offers particularly numerous examples: ambitious men whose economic campaigns were also a retreat in a forward direction.—

Actually, the scar of destitution lasts so long that those who escape from destitution do not escape from the memory of their destitution. Either by continuation or by the effect of reaction all their future life is affected by it. Some, much the greater majority, remain silent in the conservation of poverty. They are not revolutionaries. They are not equalitarians. They dwell beneath equality. A few of the others are revolutionary only for themselves. Nor are they equalitarians. They flee above equality. These are two contrary proceedings but they have the same cause: the first flee the memory of risk in the security of poverty; the second flee the memory of penury in the abundance of riches. It could be estimated that the immense majority of the once destitute thus take refuge in voluntary amnesia. Characteristic cases of this amnesia could be noted among writers, for many writers have known true destitution at the beginning of their

fugie ainsi dans des amnésies volontaires; on noterait chez
beaucoup d'écrivains des cas très caractérisés de cette amnésie, car beaucoup d'écrivains ont connu vraiment la misère
dans leurs commencements, et peu d'écrivains ont su nous
donner une exacte représentation de la misère; cette amnésie
prouverait au besoin combien la misère est grave, puisque
d'une part la mémoire de la misère demeure si vivante au
cœur des anciens misérables, et puisque d'autre part ils font
des efforts si désespérés pour échapper à cette remémoration.
Cette amnésie est pour eux comme une amnistie.

Restent ceux qui ayant par eux-mêmes la connaissance de
la misère présente ou ayant eu la connaissance de la misère
ne redoutent pas d'analyser la misère ainsi connue; misérables
ou anciens misérables, ils ont le courage de regarder la
misère en face, ils ont le courage de ne pas se réfugier dans
l'amnésie; quand ils sont engagés dans l'action, ces misérables
et ces anciens misérables se reconnaissent à des caractères
constants; mais ces caractères ne sont guère sensibles qu'à
ceux qui les ont eux-mêmes; ils sont profondément révolutionnaires, c'est-à-dire qu'ils travaillent tant qu'ils peuvent
à effectuer cette révolution de la société qui consisterait à
sauver de la misère tous les misérables sans aucune exception;
ils sont profondément socialistes, c'est-à-dire qu'ils savent
que l'on ne peut sauver des misères morales ou mentales
tant que l'on ne sauve pas de la misère économique; ils ne
sont pas égalitaires; ils ne sont pas belliqueux; ils ne sont
pas militaires; ils ne sont pas autoritaires; ils ne subissent
pas l'autorité; ils ne sont pas enthousiastes; ils ont l'admiration rare; ils évitent les cérémonies, officielles, officieuses;
ils se méfient de l'éloquence; ils redoutent l'apparat; on les
accuse, non sans apparence de raison, d'être tristes, souvent

careers and few writers have known how to give us an adequate picture of destitution. If necessary, this amnesia could prove how serious destitution is, as on the one hand the memory of destitution remains so deep-rooted in the heart of the once destitute, and on the other hand these men make such desperate efforts to escape from being reminded of it. For them, this amnesia is a sort of amnesty.

There remain those who, living in destitution or having lived in destitution and therefore knowing it intimately, do not dread the analysis of destitution thus known. Destitute or once destitute, they have the courage to look destitution in the face, they have the courage not to take refuge in amnesia. When they are engaged in action, these destitute or these once destitute recognize one another by definite characteristics. But these characteristics are scarcely perceptible save to those who possess them: they are profoundly revolutionary; that is, they work with all their might to effect that revolution of society which would consist in saving from destitution all those who are living in misery, without exception. They are profoundly socialistic; that is, they know that no man can be saved from moral or mental misery so long as he is not saved from economic destitution. They are not equalitarians. They are not bellicose. They are not military. They are not authoritative. They do not submit to authority. They are not enthusiasts. They rarely admire. They avoid formal, and informal ceremonies. They distrust eloquence. They fear pomp. Not without a semblance of reason, they are accused of being sad, often sullen. They do not appear at banquets. They neither propose nor drink toasts. The communicative warmths (of banquets) is not communicated to them. Resounding votes leave them cold. Bulletins of victory leave them in-

maussades; ils ne paraissent pas aux banquets; ils ne portent ni ne soutiennent les toasts; la chaleur communicative ne se communique pas en eux; les votes retentissants les laissent froids; les ordres du jour de victoire les laissent indifférents et perpétuellement battus; les drapeaux, même rouges, leur font mal aux yeux; les fanfares, même socialistes révolutionnaires, les étourdissent; la joie des fêtes publiques leur paraît grossière; les inaugurations pompeuses ne leur apportent pas la profonde joie des commencements et des naissances; les enterrements et les commémorations ne leur apportent pas la parfaite plénitude complète achevée de la mort; ils sont très sévères; ils ne se montent pas le coup sur la valeur des hommes et des événements; ayant une fois mesuré le monde à l'immense mesure de la misère, ils ne mesurent pas à d'autres mesures; les mesures usuelles, succès, majorité, vente, leur paraissent petites; les malheurs qui ne sont pas de la misère, insuccès, minorité, mévente, ne leur paraissent pas des malheurs sérieux; les malheurs qui ne font pas tomber ou retomber dans la misère ne leur paraissent pas des malheurs pour de bon; les bonheurs qui, dans l'ordre de l'économie, ne sont pas le bonheur d'échapper à la misère ne leur paraissent pas des bonheurs proprement dits: ce ne sont plus que des avantages, des commodités; les hommes qui n'ont pas connu comme eux la misère et qui parlent et qui sont éloquents leur paraissent toujours n'avoir pas atteint l'âge adulte, leur font l'effet d'enfants bavards; les misérables et les anciens misérables conscients ne sont pas aimés de leurs ennemis, ni de leurs camarades, mais ils sont aimés de leurs amis. Les misérables conscients ont beaucoup d'ennemis, surtout parmi leurs camarades. Mais ils ont plusieurs amis.

different and perpetually defeated. Flags, even red ones, hurt their eyes. Brass bands, even though socialist revolutionary, make them dizzy. The joy of public festivals seems vulgar to them. Pompous inaugurations do not bring them the profound joy of beginnings and births. Funerals and commemorations do not bring them the profound and complete plenitude of death. They are very austere. They do not deceive themselves as to the value of men and events. Having once measured the world by the immense measure of destitution, they do not measure with other measures. The usual measures—success, majorities, sales—seem small to them. Misfortunes which are not destitution—failure, minorities, selling at a loss—are misfortunes which do not appear serious to them. Misfortunes which do not mean falling, or falling back into destitution are not to them sure-enough misfortunes. Happiness which, in the economic order, is not the happiness of escaping destitution does not seem to them, properly speaking, happiness: it means no more than advantages, comforts. Men who have not, like themselves, known destitution and who talk and are eloquent always seem to them like garrulous children. The destitute, and those still conscious of their former destitution are not loved by their enemies, nor by their comrades, but they are loved by their friends. The consciously destitute have a great many enemies, particularly among their comrades. But they have several friends.

C'est qu'ils sont des trouble-fête. Hantés par la connaissance qu'ils ont de la misère, anxieux de savoir qu'il y a
tant de misère présente, ils ne peuvent ni ne veulent oublier
cette existence ni cette connaissance, l'espace d'un banquet,
le temps de boire au plus récent triomphe définitif de la
Révolution sociale. Donc on les hait. Ils savent que la misère n'intervient pas dans la vie comme un élément du
passif dans l'établissement d'un bilan. Ceux qui n'ont pas
connu la misère peuvent s'imaginer loyalement et logiquement que dans la vie de l'individu les éléments d'assurance
et les éléments de misère sont des éléments du même ordre,
qu'ils reçoivent la même mesure, qu'ils peuvent donc s'opposer, s'équilibrer, se balancer: nous savons qu'il n'en est
rien; les éléments de misère ont un retentissement total
sur les éléments de certitude; les éléments d'incertitude
qualifient les éléments de certitude; mais tant que la certitude n'est pas complète les éléments de certitude ne qualifient pas les éléments d'incertitude; aussi longtemps que
la certitude n'est pas complète, elle n'est pas la certitude;
une vie assurée de tous les côtés moins un n'est pas une vie
assurée; un véritable malheur, une véritable misère empoisonne toute une vie; un véritable bonheur ne peut pas
même se produire dans la misère; il y devient aussitôt
misère lui-même et malheur; il ne s'agit donc pas d'établir
un bilan de la vie individuelle où bonheur et misère seraient
équilibrés; même si on réussissait à établir ce bilan, c'est
en vain que les éléments de bonheur surpasseraient les
éléments de misère, car les éléments de bonheur n'atteignent pas les éléments de misère, et les éléments de misère
atteignent les éléments de bonheur; mais on ne peut pas
même établir ce bilan, parce que les éléments de bonheur

That is because they are kill-joys. Haunted by the knowledge of their destitution, made anxious by the knowledge of
so much present destitution, they cannot and will not forget
the existence of this destitution, nor this knowledge, for the
space of a banquet, for the time to drink to the most recent
definite triumph of the social Revolution. So they are hated.
They know that destitution does not intervene in life as does a
debit element in the drawing up of a balance sheet. Those
who have not known destitution can loyally and logically
imagine that in the life of an individual the elements of
security and the elements of destitution are elements of the
same order, that they receive the same measure, that they can
be thus opposed, balanced, counterbalanced: we know that
this is not so. The elements of destitution have a total repercussion over the elements of certainty. The elements of uncertainty qualify the elements of certainty. But as long as
certainty is not complete, the elements of certainty do not
qualify the elements of uncertainty. So long as certainty is
not complete, it is not certainty. A life secure on all sides
but one, is not secure. A real misfortune, a real destitution,
poison all of life. A real happiness cannot even take place
in destitution. There it at once becomes destitution itself, and
misfortune. So the question is not to draw up the balance
sheet of an individual life where happiness and destitution
would be in equipoise. Even if one succeeded in drawing up
this balance sheet, it would be in vain for the elements of
happiness to surpass those of destitution, for the elements
of happiness do not reach the elements of destitution and the
elements of destitution do reach the elements of happiness.
But this balance sheet cannot even be drawn up because the

et les éléments de misère ne sont pas du même ordre; et l'on ne peut pas comparer ce qui n'est pas du même ordre. Pour une vie individuelle, à l'égard de la misère, tant qu'on n'a pas fait tout, on n'a rien fait.

Ceux qui n'ont pas connu la misère peuvent s'imaginer loyalement et logiquement que dans la vie de la société les vies individuelles assurées et les vies individuelles de misère sont des unités du même ordre, qu'elles reçoivent le même compte, qu'elles peuvent donc s'opposer, s'équilibrer, se balancer; nous savons qu'il n'en est rien; les vies de misère peuvent avoir ou n'avoir pas de retentissement individuel sur les vies assurées; il reste que la misère des vies individuelles a un retentissement sur toute la vie sociale, sur la société, sur l'humanité; une cité assurée de tous les côtés moins un n'est pas une cité; un véritable malheur individuel, une véritable misère individuelle empoisonne toute une cité; une cité n'est pas fondée tant qu'elle admet une misère individuelle, quand même l'individu intéressé y consentirait; un tel consentement, un tel renoncement, recommandé dans la morale de la charité, est incompatible avec la morale de la solidarité; il ne s'agit donc pas d'établir un bilan de la vie sociale où vies individu-elles d'assurance et vies individuelles de misère seraient équilibrées; même si on réussissait à établir ce bilan, c'est en vain que les vies de bonheur surpasseraient en nombre, en quantité, les vies de misère, car les vies de bonheur n'atteignent pas les vies de misère et les vies de misère atteignent les vies de bonheur; mais on ne peut pas même établir ce bilan, parce que les vies de bonheur et les vies de misère ne sont pas du même ordre; on ne peut les comparer. Pour la vie sociale, à l'égard de la misère, tant qu'on n'a pas fait tout, on n'a rien fait.

elements of happiness and those of destitution are not of the same order. And things not of the same order cannot be compared. As for destitution, in an individual life, as long as one has not done all, one has done nothing.

Those who have not known destitution can loyally and logically imagine that in the life of society, secure individual lives and individual lives of destitution are units of the same order; that they receive the same settlement, that they can thus be opposed, balanced, counterbalanced. We know that this is not so. Lives of destitution may, or may not have an individual repercussion on secure lives. It remains that the destitution of individual lives has a repercussion on all social life, on society, on humanity. A city secure on all sides but one is not a city. A real individual misfortune, a real individual destitution poison a whole city. A city is not founded so long as it admits of an individual destitution, even though the individual involved would consent to it. Such a consent, such a renouncement, recommended by the morality of charity, is incompatible with the morality of solidarity. So the question is not to draw up a balance sheet of social life where secure individual lives and individual lives of destitution would find their equipoise. Even if one succeeded in drawing up this balance sheet, it would be in vain for lives of happiness to surpass in number and quota the lives of destitution, for the lives of happiness do not reach the lives of destitution whereas the lives of destitution do reach the lives of happiness. But this balance sheet cannot even be drawn up because the lives of happiness and the lives of destitution are not of the same order. They cannot be compared. As for destitution, in social life, so long as one has not done all, one has done nothing.

L'HONNEUR DU TRAVAIL

NOUS AVONS CONNU, nous avons touché l'ancienne France et nous l'avons connue intacte. Nous en avons été enfants. —

Nous essaierons, si nous le pouvons, de représenter cela. — Le monde a moins changé depuis Jésus-Christ qu'il n'a changé depuis trente ans. Il y a eu l'âge antique (et biblique). Il y a eu l'âge chrétien. Il y a l'âge moderne. Une ferme en Beauce, encore après la guerre, était infiniment plus près d'une ferme gallo-romaine, ou plutôt de la même ferme gallo-romaine, pour les mœurs, pour le statut, pour le sérieux, pour la gravité, pour la structure même et l'institution, pour la dignité, (et même, au fond, d'une ferme de Xénophon), qu'aujourd'hui elle ne se ressemble à elle-même. Nous essaierons de le dire. Nous avons connu un temps où quand une bonne femme disait un mot, c'était sa race même, son être, son peuple qui parlait. Qui sortait. Et quand un ouvrier allumait sa cigarette, ce qu'il allait vous dire, ce n'était pas ce que le journaliste a dit dans le journal de ce matin. Les libres-penseurs de ce temps-là étaient plus chrétiens que nos dévots d'aujourd'hui. Une paroisse ordinaire de ce temps-là était

THE HONOR OF WORK

W E HAVE KNOWN, we have touched bygone France and we have known her unimpaired. We have been her children.—

We will try, if we can, to present this.—The world has changed less since Jesus Christ than it has in the last thirty years.* There was the age of antiquity (and of the Bible). There was the Christian age. There is the modern age. Even after the war **, a farm in the Beauce country resembled a farm of the Gallo-Roman age infinitely more than this same farm resembles itself today. Or rather, this farm was like its Gallo-Roman self, as far as customs, regulations, serious-ness, gravity, in structure itself, in institution and in dignity. (And even, at bottom, it was close to a farm of the time of Xenophon.) We will try to explain this. We have known the time when, if a simple woman uttered a word, it was her race itself, her being, her people, which spoke, which came out. And when a workman lit his cigarette, what he was about to tell you was not what a journalist had said in that morning's paper. The freethinkers of that time were more Christian than are our devout people of today. An average parish of

---

*1913.
** The war of 1870.

infiniment plus près d'une paroisse du quinzième siècle, ou
du quatrième siècle, mettons du cinquième ou du huitième,
que d'une paroisse actuelle. —

Le croira-t-on, nous avons été nourris dans un peuple gai.
Dans ce temps-là un chantier était un lieu de la terre où des
hommes étaient heureux. Aujourd'hui un chantier est un lieu
de la terre ou des hommes récriminent, s'en veulent, se battent ; se tuent.

De mon temps tout le monde chantait. (Excepté moi, mais
j'étais déjà indigne d'être de ce temps-là). Dans la plupart
des corps de métiers on chantait. Aujourd'hui on renâcle.
Dans ce temps-là on ne gagnait pour ainsi dire rien. Les
salaires étaient d'une bassesse dont on n'a pas idée. Et pourtant tout le monde bouffait. Il y avait dans les plus humbles
maisons une sorte d'aisance dont on a perdu le souvenir. Au
fond on ne comptait pas. Et on n'avait pas à compter. Et on
pouvait élever des enfants. Et on en élevait. Il n'y avait pas
cette espèce d'affreuse strangulation économique qui à présent
d'année en année nous donne un tour de plus. On ne gagnait
rien; on ne dépensait rien; et tout le monde vivait.

Il n'y avait pas cet étranglement économique d'aujourd'hui,
cette strangulation scientifique, froide, rectangulaire, régu-
lière, propre, nette, sans une bavure, implacable, sage, commune, constante, commode comme une vertu, où il n'y a rien
à dire, et où celui qui est étranglé a si évidemment tort.

On ne saura jamais jusqu'où allait la décence et la justesse
d'âme de ce peuple; une telle finesse, une telle culture profonde ne se retrouvera plus. Ni une telle finesse et précaution
de parler. Ces gens-là eussent rougi de notre meilleur ton
d'aujourd'hui, qui est le ton bourgeois. Et aujourd'hui tout
le monde est bourgeois.

that time was infinitely closer to a fifteenth century parish, or one of the fourth century—or let us say one of the fifth or eighth centuries—than to one of our present-day parishes.—

Believe it if you can, we were fostered among a gay people. In those days a workyard was a spot on earth where men were happy. Today a workyard is a spot on earth where men find fault, wish each other ill, fight; kill each other.

In my day everybody sang (myself excepted, but I was already unworthy to belong to those times). In most of the corporations, one sang. Today, one balks. In those days, one earned scarcely anything, so to speak. No one has any idea how low salaries were. And yet everyone had enough grub. In the humblest cottages reigned a sort of ease, the memory of which is lost. At bottom, no one reckoned. And there was nothing to reckon about. And children could be reared. And they were reared. This atrocious economic strangulation which year by year tightens its grip on us did not exist. One earned nothing. One spent nothing. And everybody lived.

The economic strangulation of today, that scientific, cold, rectangular, regular, clean, clearcut, seamless, implacable, wise, common, constant, convenient-as-a-virtue strangulation; that strangulation where there is nothing to be said and where the strangled one is so obviously in the wrong, did not exist.

We will never know the true extent of the decency and truthfulness of this people's soul. Such delicacy, such deep culture will never more be found. Nor such a delicacy and cautiousness of speech. The people of those days would have blushed for our best tone of today, which is the bourgeois tone. And today, everyone is bourgeois.

Nous croira-t-on, et ceci revient encore au même, nous avons connu des ouvriers qui avaient envie de travailler. On ne pensait qu'à travailler. Nous avons connu des ouvriers qui le matin ne pensaient qu'à travailler. Ils se levaient le matin, et à quelle heure, et ils chantaient à l'idée qu'ils partaient travailler. A onze heures ils chantaient en allant à la soupe. — Travailler était leur joie même, et la racine profonde de leur être. Et la raison de leur être. Il y avait un honneur incroyable du travail, le plus beau de tous les honneurs, le plus chrétien, le seul peut-être qui se tienne debout. C'est par exemple pour cela que je dis qu'un libre-penseur de ce temps-là était plus chrétien qu'un dévot de nos jours. Parce qu'un dévot de nos jours est forcément un bourgeois. Et aujourd'hui tout le monde est bourgeois.

Nous avons connu un honneur du travail exactement le même que celui qui au moyen-âge régissait la main et le cœur. C'était le même conservé intact en dessous. Nous avons connu ce soin poussé jusqu'à la perfection, égal dans l'ensemble, égal dans le plus infime détail. Nous avons connu cette piété de *l'ouvrage bien faite* poussée, maintenue jusqu'à ses plus extrêmes exigences. J'ai vu toute mon enfance rempailler des chaises exactement du même esprit et du même cœur, et de la même main, que ce même peuple avait taillé ses cathédrales.

Que reste-t-il aujourd'hui de tout cela ? Comment a-t-on fait, du peuple le plus laborieux de la terre, et peut-être du seul peuple laborieux de la terre, du seul peuple peut-être qui aimait le travail pour le travail, et pour l'honneur, et pour travailler, ce peuple de saboteurs, comment a-t-on pu en faire ce peuple qui sur un chantier met toute son étude à ne pas en fiche un coup. Ce sera dans l'histoire une des plus

Can we be believed?—and once more this amounts to the
same—we have known workmen who really wanted to work.
No one thought of anything but work. We have known workmen who in the morning thought of nothing but work. They
got up in the morning (and at what an hour), and they sang
at the idea that they were off to work. At eleven o'clock they
sang on going off to eat their soup.—Work for them was joy
itself and the deep root of their being. And the reason of
their being. There was an incredible honor in work, the most
beautiful of all the honors, the most Christian, perhaps the
only one which stands of itself. That is why I say, for example, that a freethinker of those days was more Christian
than a devout person of our day. Because nowadays a devout
person is perforce a bourgeois. And today, everyone is
bourgeois.

We have known an honor of work exactly similar to that
which in the Middle Ages ruled hand and heart. The same
honor had been preserved, intact underneath. We have known
this care carried to perfection, a perfect whole, perfect to the
last infinitesimal detail. We have known this devotion to
l'ouvrage bien faite, to the good job, carried and maintained
to its most exacting claims. During all my childhood I saw
chairs being caned exactly in the same spirit, with the same
hand and heart as those with which this same people fash-
ioned its cathedrals.

Today, what remains of all this? How has the most laborious people on earth, and perhaps the only laborious people
on earth, perhaps the only people that loved work for work's
sake, and for honor, or in a word, just loved to work, been
changed into this people of saboteurs? How has this people
been transformed into one which in the workyard takes the

grandes victoires, et sans doute la seule, de la démagogie bourgeoise intellectuelle. Mais il faut avouer qu'elle compte. Cette victoire.

Il y a eu la révolution chrétienne. Et il y a eu la révolution moderne. Voilà les deux qu'il faut compter. Un artisan de mon temps était un artisan de n'importe quel temps chrétien. Et sans doute peut-être de n'importe quel temps antique. Un artisan d'aujourd'hui n'est plus un artisan.

Dans ce bel honneur de métier convergeaient tous les plus beaux, tous les plus nobles sentiments. Une dignité. Une fierté. *Ne jamais rien demander à personne*, disaient-ils. Voilà dans quelles idées nous avons été élevés. Car demander du travail, ce n'était pas demander. C'était le plus normalement du monde, le plus naturellement réclamer, pas même réclamer. C'était se mettre à sa place dans un atelier. C'était, dans une cité laborieuse, se mettre tranquillement à la place de travail qui vous attendait. Un ouvrier de ce temps-là ne savait pas ce que c'est que quémander. C'est la bourgeoisie qui quémande. C'est la bourgeoisie qui, les faisant bourgeois, leur a appris a quémander. Aujourd'hui dans cette insolence même et dans cette brutalité, dans cette sorte d'incohérence qu'ils apportent à leurs revendications il est très facile de sentir cette honte sourde, d'être forcés de demander, d'avoir été amenés, par l'événement de l'histoire économique, à quémander. Ah oui ils demandent quelque chose à quelqu'un, à présent. Ils demandent même tout à tout le monde. Exiger, c'est encore demander. C'est encore servir.

Ces ouvriers ne servaient pas. Ils travaillaient. Ils avaient un honneur, absolu, comme c'est le propre d'un honneur. Il fallait qu'un bâton de chaise fût bien fait. C'était entendu. C'était un primat. Il ne fallait pas qu'il fût bien fait pour le

greatest pains not to lift a hand? In history, this will be one of the greatest victories, and doubtless the only one, of the intellectual bourgeois demagogy. But we must admit that it counts, this victory.

There was the Christian revolution. And there was the modern revolution. These are the two revolutions that we must count. In my day, an artisan was an artisan belonging to any Christian time. And doubtless to any time in antiquity. Today, an artisan is no longer an artisan.

Towards this fine honor of a trade converged all the finest, all the most noble sentiments—dignity, pride. *Never ask anything of anyone,* they used to say. These are the ideas in which we were brought up. For to ask for work was not to ask. The most normal, most natural thing in the world to claim, not even to claim, was to take one's place in a workroom, in a working city, quietly to take one's place before the work which awaited one. In those days a workman did not know what it was to solicit. It is the bourgeoisie who solicit. It is the bourgeoisie who, turning the workmen into bourgeois, have taught them to solicit. Today in this same insolence and in this brutality, in the sort of incoherence which they bring into their demands, it is very easy to sense this hidden shame of being forced to ask, of having been brought, by the new laws of economic history, to solicit. Oh yes, they ask something of someone, nowadays. They even ask everything of everyone. To exact is still to ask. It is still to serve.

Those bygone workmen did not serve, they worked. They had an absolute honor, which is honor proper. A chair rung had to be well made. That was an understood thing. That was the first thing. It wasn't that the chair rung had to be

salaire ou moyennant le salaire. Il ne fallait pas qu'il fût
bien fait pour le patron ni pour les connaisseurs ni pour les
clients du patron. Il fallait qu'il fût bien fait lui-même, en
lui-même, pour lui-même, dans son être même. Une tradition,
venue, montée du plus profond de la race, une histoire, un
absolu, un honneur voulait que ce bâton de chaise fût bien
fait. Toute partie, dans la chaise, qui ne se voyait pas, était
exactement aussi parfaitement faite que ce qu'on voyait. C'est
le principe même des cathédrales.

Et encore c'est moi qui en cherche si long, moi dégénéré.
Pour eux, chez eux il n'y avait pas l'ombre d'une réflexion.
Le travail était là. On travaillait bien.

Il ne s'agissait pas d'être vu ou pas vu. C'était l'être même
du travail qui devait être bien fait.

Et un sentiment incroyablement profond de ce que nous
nommons aujourd'hui l'honneur du sport, mais en ce temps-là
répandu partout. Non seulement l'idée de faire rendre le
mieux, mais l'idée, dans le mieux, dans le bien, de faire
rendre le plus. Non seulement à qui ferait le mieux, mais à
qui en ferait le plus, c'était un beau sport continuel, qui était
de toutes les heures, dont la vie même était pénétrée. Tissée.
Un dégoût sans fond pour l'ouvrage mal fait. Un mépris plus
que de grand seigneur pour celui qui eût mal travaillé. Mais
l'idée ne leur en venait même pas.

Tous les honneurs convergeaient en cet honneur. Une décence, et une finesse de langage. Un respect du foyer. Un sens
du respect, de tous les respects, de l'être même du respect.
Une cérémonie pour ainsi dire constante. D'ailleurs le foyer
se confondait encore très souvent avec l'atelier et l'honneur
du foyer et l'honneur de l'atelier était le même honneur.
C'était l'honneur du même lieu. C'était l'honneur du même

well made for the salary or on account of the salary. It wasn't
that it was well made for the boss, nor for connaisseurs, nor
for the boss' clients. It had to be well made itself, in itself,
for itself, in its very self. A tradition coming, springing from
deep within the race, a history, an absolute, an honor, de-
manded that this chair rung be well made. Every part of the
chair which could not be seen was just as perfectly made as
the parts which could be seen. This was the selfsame principle of cathedrals.

And once again, it is I who seek out these lengthy reasons,
I who have degenerated. For them, in their homes, there was
not the shadow of a doubt. The work was there. One worked
well.

There was no question of being seen or of not being seen.
It was the innate being of work which needed to be well
done.

And there was an incredibly deep feeling of what we now
call the honor of sport, but which in those days flourished
everywhere. Not only the idea of producing the best, but in
the best, the idea of producing the most. Not only to vie as
to who could do the best but also as to who could do the most
was the fine uninterrupted sport of every hour, which pene-
trated all of life, was woven into it. A bottomless disgust for
bad workmanship, a more than lordly contempt for him who
worked badly. But that idea didn't even occur to them.

All the honors converged towards that honor. A decency
and a delicacy of speech. A respect for home. A sense of respects, of all the respects, of respect itself. A constant ceremony, as it were. Besides, home was still very often iden-
tified with the work-room, and the honor of home and the
honor of the work-room were the same honor. It was the

feu. Qu'est-ce que tout cela est devenu ? Tout était un rythme et un rite et une cérémonie depuis le petit lever. Tout était un événement; sacré. Tout était une tradition, un enseignement, tout était légué, tout était la plus sainte habitude. Tout était une élévation, intérieure, et une prière, toute la journée, le sommeil et la veille, le travail et le peu de repos, le lit et la table, la soupe et le bœuf, la maison et le jardin, la porte et la rue, la cour et le pas de porte, et les assiettes sur la table.

Ils disaient en riant, et pour embêter les curés, que *travailler c'est prier*, et ils ne croyaient pas si bien dire.

Tant leur travail était une prière. Et l'atelier était un oratoire.

Tout était le long événement d'un beau rite. Ils eussent été bien surpris, ces ouvriers, et quel eût été, non pas même leur dégoût, leur incrédulité, comme ils auraient cru que l'on blaguait, si on leur avait dit que quelques années plus tard, dans les chantiers, les ouvriers, — les compagnons, — se proposeraient officiellement d'en faire le moins possible; et qu'ils considéreraient ça comme une grande victoire. Une telle idée pour eux, en supposant qu'ils la pussent concevoir, c'eût été porter une atteinte directe à eux-mêmes, à leur être, ç'aurait été douter de leur capacité, puisque ç'aurait été supposer qu'ils ne rendraient pas tant qu'ils pouvaient. C'est comme de supposer d'un soldat qu'il ne sera pas victorieux.

Eux aussi ils vivaient dans une victoire perpétuelle, mais quelle autre victoire. Quelle même et quelle autre. Une victoire de toutes les heures du jour dans tous les jours de la vie. Un honneur égal à n'importe quel honneur militaire. Les sentiments mêmes de la garde impériale.

honor of the same place. It was the honor of the same hearth.
What has become of all this? Everything was a rhythm and
a rite and a ceremony from the moment of rising in the early
morning. Everything was an event; a sacred event. Everything was a tradition, a lesson, everything was bequeathed,
everything was a most saintly habit. Everything was an inner
elevation and a prayer. All day long, sleep and wake, work
and short rest, bed and board, soup and beef, house and
garden, door and street, courtyard and threshold, and the
plates on the table.

Laughing, they used to say, and that to annoy the priests,
that *to work is to pray* and little did they know how true
that was.

So much of their work was a prayer, and the work-room
an oratory.

Everything was the long event of a beautiful rite. These
workmen would have been much surprised and what would
have been—not even their disgust, their incredulity—if they
had been told that a few years later in the workyards, the
workmen, the journeymen, would officially propose to do as
little as possible. And that they would consider this a great
victory. Such an idea, supposing that they could conceive of
such a thing, would have struck directly at them, at their
being. It would have been a doubt cast upon their capacity,
for it would have inferred that they did not do as much as
they could. It is like supposing of a soldier that he will not be
victorious.

They too lived in a perpetual victory, but what a victory!
How much the same and yet how different! A victory every
hour of the day, every day of life. An honor equal to no
matter what military honor. The selfsame sentiments of the
imperial guard.

Et par suite ou ensemble tous les beaux sentiments adjoints ou connexes, tous les beaux sentiments dérivés et filiaux. Un respect des vieillards; des parents, de la parenté. Un admirable respect des enfants. Naturellement un respect de la femme. (Et il faut bien le dire, puisque aujourd'hui c'est cela qui manque tant, un respect de la femme par la femme elle-même). Un respect de la famille, un respect du foyer. Et surtout un goût propre et un respect du respect même. Un respect de l'outil, et de la main, ce suprême outil. *Je perds ma main à travailler,* disaient les vieux. Et c'était la fin des fins. L'idée qu'on aurait pu abîmer ses outils exprès ne leur eût pas même semblé le dernier des sacrilèges. Elle ne leur eût pas même semblé la pire des folies. Elle ne leur eût pas même semblé monstrueuse. Elle leur eût semblé la supposition la plus extravagante. C'eût été comme si on leur eût parlé de se couper la main. L'outil n'était qu'une main plus longue, ou plus dure, (des ongles d'acier), ou plus particulièrement affectée. Une main qu'on s'était faite exprès pour ceci ou pour cela.

Un ouvrier abîmer un outil, pour eux, c'eût été, dans cette guerre, le conscrit qui se coupe le pouce.

On ne gagnait rien, on vivait de rien, on était heureux. Il ne s'agit pas là-dessus de se livrer à des arithmétiques de sociologue. C'est un fait, un des rares faits que nous connaissions, que nous ayons pu embrasser, un des rares faits dont nous puissions témoigner, un des rares faits qui soit incontestable.

On ne peut se représenter quelle était alors la santé de cette race. Et surtout, cette bonne humeur, générale, constante, ce climat de bonne humeur. Et ce bonheur, ce climat de bonheur. Evidemment on ne vivait point encore dans l'égalité. On n'y pensait même pas, à l'égalité, j'entends à une égalité

And successively, or together, all the beautiful adjoining or connected sentiments, all the beautiful sentiments derived or filial. A respect for the aged; for parents, for kinship. An admirable respect for children. Naturally a respect for womanhood. (And it must be said, since today this is so sadly lacking, a respect of woman herself for womanhood.) A respect for family, a respect for home. And above all, an innate feeling for respect and a respect for respect itself. A respect for the tool and for the hand, that supreme tool. *My hand loses its cunning,* the old men used to say. And that was the end of everything. The idea that anyone could purposely damage his tool would not even have appeared to them the ultimate sacrilege. It would not even have appeared to them as the crowning madness. It would not have appeared to them as a monstrous crime. To them it would have appeared the most extravagant of assumptions. It would have been as though someone had suggested their cutting off a hand. A tool was merely a longer or harder hand (steel nails) or one more specially affected, a hand which you yourself had made expressly for this or that purpose.

A workman who damaged a tool would have been to them like a conscript who, during a war, cuts off his thumb.

You earned nothing, you lived on nothing, you were happy. The question here has nothing to do with enlarging upon social arithmetic. It is a fact, one of the rare facts which we know, which we have been able to embrace, one of the rare facts to which we can bear witness, one of the rare facts which are unquestionable.

One cannot imagine what the health of the race was, then. And above all that good humor, general, constant, that atmosphere of good humor. Obviously one didn't yet live in

sociale. Une inégalité commune, communément acceptée, une inégalité générale, un ordre, une hiérarchie qui paraissait naturelle ne faisaient qu'étager les différents niveaux d'un commun bonheur. On ne parle aujourd'hui que de l'égalité. Et nous vivons dans la plus monstrueuse inégalité économique que l'on ait jamais vue dans l'histoire du monde. On vivait alors. On avait des enfants. Ils n'avaient aucunement cette impression que nous avons d'être au bagne. Ils n'avaient pas comme nous cette impression d'un étranglement économique, d'un collier de fer qui tient à la gorge et qui se serre tous les jours d'un cran. Ils n'avaient point inventé cet admirable mécanisme de la grève moderne à jet continu, qui fait toujours monter les salaires d'un tiers, et le prix de la vie d'une bonne moitié, et la misère, de la différence. —

Notez qu'aujourd'hui au fond ça ne les amuse pas de ne rien faire sur les chantiers. Ils aimeraient mieux travailler. Ils ne sont pas en vain de cette race laborieuse. Ils entendent cet appel de la race. La main qui démange, qui a envie de travailler. Le bras qui s'embête, de ne rien faire. Le sang qui court dans les veines. La tête qui travaille et qui par une sorte de convoitise, anticipée, par une sorte de préemption, par une véritable anticipation s'empare d'avance de l'ouvrage fait. Comme leurs pères ils entendent ce sourd appel du travail qui veut être fait. Et au fond ils se dégoûtent d'eux-mêmes, d'abîmer les outils. Mais voilà, des messieurs très bien, des savants, des bourgeois leur ont expliqué que c'était ça le socialisme, et que c'était ça la révolution.

equality. One didn't even think of equality, I mean of social equality. A common inequality, commonly accepted, a general inequality, an order, a hierarchy which appeared natural because it only meant the different levels of a common happiness. Nowadays, nothing is spoken of but equality. And we live in the most monstrous economic inequality that has ever been seen in the history of the world. In those days, one lived. One had children. Then, no one had the impression that we have of living in penal servitude. No one had then, as we have now, the impression of economic strangulation, of an iron collar tightening around the throat, each day a little tighter. No one then had invented that admirable mechanism of the modern strike, in an unbroken stream, which always makes salaries rise by a third, and the cost of living by a good half—and the resulting destitution caused by the difference between the two levels.—

Note that, at bottom, it doesn't amuse workmen today to do nothing in the workyards. They would prefer to work. It is not in vain that they belong to a laborious race. They hear the call of this race. The hand that itches, that wants to work. The arm that is bored with nothing to do. The blood that courses through the veins. The head that seethes and which, with a sort of anticipated covetousness, by a sort of preemption, by a real anticipation, seizes ahead of time the finished work. Like their fathers they hear the muffled call of work that wishes to be done. And at bottom, they are disgusted with themselves for damaging their tools. But there you are, highly respectable gentlemen, the scholars, the bourgeois, have explained to them that this was socialism and that this was the revolution.

Car on ne saurait trop le redire. Tout le mal est venu de la bourgeoisie. Toute l'aberration, tout le crime. C'est la bourgeoisie capitaliste qui a infecté le peuple. Et elle l'a précisément infecté d'esprit bourgeois et capitaliste.

Je dis expressément la bourgeoisie capitaliste et la grosse bourgeoisie. La bourgeoisie laborieuse au contraire, la petite bourgeoisie est devenue la classe la plus malheureuse de toutes les classes sociales, la seule aujourd'hui qui travaille réellement, la seule qui par suite ait conservé intactes les vertus ouvrières, et pour sa récompense la seule enfin qui vive réellement dans la misère. Elle seule a tenu le coup, on se demande par quel miracle, elle seule tient encore le coup, et s'il y a quelque rétablissement, c'est que c'est elle qui aura conservé le statut.

Ainsi les ouvriers n'ont point conservé les vertus ouvrières; et c'est la petite bourgeoisie qui les a conservées.

La bourgeoisie capitaliste par contre a tout infecté. Elle s'est infectée elle-même et elle a infecté le peuple, de la même infection. —

Si la bourgeoisie était demeurée non pas tant peut-être ce qu'elle était que ce qu'elle avait à être et ce qu'elle pouvait être, l'arbitre économique de la valeur qui se vend, la classe ouvrière ne demandait qu'à demeurer ce qu'elle avait toujours été, la source économique de la valeur qui se vend.

On ne saurait trop le redire, c'est la bourgeoisie qui a commencé à saboter et tout le sabotage a pris naissance dans la bourgeoisie. C'est parce que la bourgeoisie s'est mise à traiter comme une valeur de bourse le travail de l'homme que le travailleur s'est mis, lui aussi, à traiter comme une valeur de bourse son propre travail. C'est parce que la bourgeoisie s'est mise à faire perpétuellement des coups de bourse sur le

For it cannot be repeated too often: all the evil, all the aberration, all the crime has come from the bourgeoisie. It is the capitalistic bourgeoisie which has infected the people. And it has infected them precisely with the bourgeois and capitalistic spirit.

I say expressly the capitalistic bourgeoisie and the upper bourgeoisie. The laborious lower bourgeoisie, on the other hand, have become the most unhappy of all social classes, the only one today which really works, consequently the only one which has preserved untouched the virtues of the working classes, and which, as a reward, is the only one which lives in real destitution. The small bourgeoisie alone has held tight, one wonders by what miracle it alone has held tight, and if some sort of re-establishment should take place, this class alone will have preserved the statutes.

So the workers have not preserved the virtues of the working classes; it is the small bourgeoisie who have preserved them.

The capitalistic bourgeoisie on the other hand has infected everything. It has infected itself and it has infected the people with the same infection.—

If the bourgeoisie had remained not so much what she was, perhaps, as what she ought to have been and what she could have been, the economic umpire of securities which are sold, the working class would have asked nothing better than to remain what it has always been: the economic source of securities which are sold.

It cannot be repeated too often that it is the bourgeoisie who began the sabotage and all sabotage took birth in the bourgeoisie. This is because the bourgeoisie began to treat the work of man as a security on the stock exchange. And

travail de l'homme que le travailleur, lui aussi, par imitation, par collusion et encontre, et on pourrait presque dire par entente, s'est mis à faire continuellement des coups de bourse sur son propre travail. C'est parce que la bourgeoisie s'est mise à exercer un chantage perpétuel sur le travail de l'homme que nous vivons sous ce régime de coups de bourse et de chantage perpétuel que sont notamment les grèves: Ainsi est disparue cette notion du juste prix, dont nos intellectuels bourgeois font aujourd'hui des gorges chaudes, mais qui n'en a pas moins été le durable fondement de tout un monde.

Car, et c'est ici la deuxième et la non moins redoutable infection: en même temps que la bourgeoisie introduisait et pratiquait en grand le sabotage pour son propre compte, en même temps elle introduisait dans le monde ouvrier les théoriciens patentés du sabotage. En même temps qu'en face elle en donnait l'exemple et le modèle, en même temps dedans elle en donnait l'enseignement. Le parti *politique* socialiste est entièrement composé de bourgeois intellectuels. Ce sont eux qui ont inventé le sabotage et la double désertion, la déser-tion du travail, la désertion de l'outil. Pour ne point parler ici de la désertion militaire, qui est un cas particulier de la grande désertion, comme la gloire militaire était un cas particulier de la grande gloire. Ce sont eux qui ont fait croire au peuple que c'était cela le socialisme et que c'était cela la révolution.

that is also why the worker in his turn began to treat his own work as a security on the stock exchange. It is because the bourgeoisie set about speculating perpetually on the work of man in the stock exchange that the workman too, in imitation, collusion and opposition, and one could almost say by agreement, set about speculating perpetually on his own work. It is because the bourgeoisie began to exert perpetual blackmail over the work of man that we live in this regime of speculation and perpetual blackmail. These are, notably, strikes. Thus the notion of a just price has disappeared, this notion at which our intellectual bourgeois laugh so heartily today but which was, nevertheless, the durable foundation of an entire world.

For, and this is the second and no less dreadful infection: at the time when the bourgeoisie introduced and practised sabotage on a grand scale on her own account, she introduced at the same time the patented theorists of sabotage into the working man's world. While the bourgeoisie was openly giving the example and the model, at the same time, and underhandedly, she was giving the lesson. The *political* socialist party is entirely composed of intellectual bourgeois. They are those who invented sabotage and the double desertion, the desertion from work and the desertion from tools. Not to mention here military desertion, which is a particular instance of the great desertion, just as military glory was a particular instance of the great glory. It is the bourgeoisie who have made the people believe that this was socialism and that this was the revolution.

LES INSTITUTEURS

IL NE FAUT PAS que l'instituteur soit dans la commune le représentant du gouvernement; il convient qu'il y soit le représentant de l'humanité; ce n'est pas un président du conseil, si considérable que soit un président du conseil, ce n'est pas une majorité qu'il faut que l'instituteur dans la commune représente: il est le représentant né de personnages moins transitoires, il est le seul et l'inestimable représentant des poètes et des artistes, des philosophes et des savants, des hommes qui ont fait et qui maintiennent l'humanité. Il doit assurer la représentation de la culture. C'est pour cela qu'il ne peut pas assumer la représentation de la politique, parce qu'il ne peut pas cumuler les deux représentations.

Mais pour cela, et nous devons avoir le courage de le répéter aux instituteurs, il est indispensable qu'ils se cultivent eux-mêmes; il ne s'agit pas d'enseigner à tort et à travers; il faut savoir ce que l'on enseigne, c'est-à-dire qu'il faut avoir commencé par s'enseigner soi-même; les hommes les plus éminents ne cessent pas de se cultiver, ou plutôt les hommes les plus éminents sont ceux qui n'ont pas cessé, qui ne cessent pas de se cultiver, de travailler; on n'a rien sans peine, et la

THE SCHOOLTEACHERS

I N A COMMUNITY, the schoolteacher must not be the representative of the government. It is fitting that he should be the representative of humanity. It is not a prime minister, no matter how important a prime minister may be; it is not a majority that the schoolteacher should represent in the community. He is the born representative of less fleeting personages, he is the only and priceless representative of poets and artists, of philosophers and scholars, of the men who have made and maintained humanity. He must ensure the representation of culture. That is why he cannot assume the representation of politics, because he cannot hold two offices, two representations.

If this is to be, we must have the courage to repeat to schoolteachers how indispensable it is that they should cultivate themselves. To teach at random is not the question. One must know what one teaches, that is, one must have begun by first teaching oneself. The most eminent men never cease cultivating themselves; or rather, the most eminent men are those who have never ceased, who ceaselessly continue their culture, their work. Nothing is obtained without pains, and

vie est un perpétuel travail. — L'enseignement ne se confère pas: il se travaille, et se communique. — C'est en lisant qu'un homme se forme, et non pas en récitant des manuels. Et c'est, aussi, en travaillant, modestement.

CE N'EST POINT par l'horreur du laid mais par l'attrait du beau que nous devons enseigner le beau. Le beau doit ignorer le laid comme le Dieu d'Aristote ignorait le monde imparfait.

QUAND ON REND LES ENFANTS MALHEUREUX, on est un criminel et on risque de les tuer. Quand on les rend heureux, on a raison, mais on risque de les rendre niais, présomptueux, insolents.

ENSEIGNER à lire, telle serait la seule et la véritable fin d'un enseignement bien entendu; que le lecteur sache lire et tout est sauvé.

C'EST UNE ILLUSION DANGEREUSE que de croire que l'on peut publier sans recevoir, écrire sans lire, parler sans écouter, produire sans se nourrir, donner de soi sans se refaire.

life is perpetual work.—Education cannot be conferred: it is obtained by work, and is communicated.—It is by reading that a man shapes himself and not by reciting handbooks. And it is also by working modestly.

WE MUST TEACH beauty not from horror of ugliness but rather by attraction to beauty. Beauty should ignore ugliness as the God of Aristotle ignored an imperfect world.

WHEN ONE MAKES CHILDREN UNHAPPY one is a criminal and risks killing them. When one makes them happy, one is right, while running the risk of making them silly, presumptuous, insolent.

TEACHING PEOPLE to read, such would be the sole and true end of a skilful education; let the reader know how to read and all is saved.

IT IS A DANGEROUS ILLUSION to believe that one can publish without receiving, write without reading, talk without listening, produce without feeding oneself, to give of oneself without recovering one's strength.

LE MONDE MODERNE

Politique et Mystique

Le socialisme et le monde moderne

L'avenir

THE MODERN WORLD

POLITIQUE ET MYSTIQUE

Nous sommes les derniers. Presque les après-derniers. Aussitôt après nous commence un autre âge, un tout autre monde, le monde de ceux qui ne croient plus à rien, qui s'en font gloire et orgueil.

Aussitôt après nous commence le monde que nous avons nommé, que nous ne cesserons pas de nommer le monde moderne. Le monde qui fait le malin. Le monde des intelligents, des avancés, de ceux qui savent, de ceux à qui on n'en remontre pas, de ceux à qui on n'en fait pas accroire. Le monde de ceux à qui on n'a plus rien à apprendre. Le monde de ceux qui font le malin. Le monde de ceux qui ne sont pas des dupes, des imbéciles. Comme nous. C'est-à-dire: le monde de ceux qui ne croient à rien, pas même à l'athéisme, qui ne se dévouent, qui ne se sacrifient à rien. Exactement: le monde de ceux qui n'ont pas de mystique. Et qui s'en vantent. Qu'on ne s'y trompe pas, et que personne par conséquent ne se réjouisse, ni d'un côté ni de l'autre. Le mouvement de dérépublicanisation de la France est profondément le même mouvement que le mouvement de sa déchristianisation. C'est ensemble un même, un seul mouvement profond de démysti-

POLITICS AND MYSTICISM

W̶E ARE THE LAST. Almost beyond the last. Immediately after us begins another age, a quite different world, the world of those who no longer believe in anything; those for whom this is a source of pride and glory.

Immediately after us begins the world which we have just mentioned, that which we will not cease to call the modern world; the world of the know-alls; the world of the intelligent, the advanced, of those who know, of those who can't be taught a thing, of those who can't be fooled: the world of those to whom there is nothing left to teach. The world of the know-alls. The world of those who are neither dupes nor imbeciles, like us. That is: the world of those who believe in nothing, not even in atheism, who show neither devotion nor sacrifice for anything. Exactly this: the world of those who have no mysticism; and who boast of it. Let us not be misled and consequently, let no one rejoice, on one side or the other. The movement for de-republicanizing France is profoundly the same movement as the movement which de-Christianized her. All-in-all it is a same, a single profound movement against mysticism. It is of a same profound movement that

cation. C'est du même mouvement profond, d'un seul mouvement, que ce peuple ne croit plus à la République et qu'il ne croit plus à Dieu, qu'il ne veut plus mener la vie républicaine, et qu'il ne veut plus mener la vie chrétienne, (qu'il en a assez), on pourrait presque dire qu'il ne veut plus croire aux idoles et qu'il ne veut plus croire au vrai Dieu. La même incrédulité, une seule incrédulité atteint les idoles et Dieu, atteint ensemble les faux dieux et le vrai Dieu, les dieux antiques, le Dieu nouveau, les dieux anciens et le Dieu des chrétiens. Une même stérilité dessèche la cité et la chrétienté. La cité politique et la cité chrétienne. La cité des hommes et la cité de Dieu. C'est proprement la stérilité moderne. Que nul donc ne se réjouisse, voyant le malheur qui arrive à l'ennemi, à l'adversaire, au voisin. Car le même malheur, la même stérilité lui arrive.

Je ne dis point que c'est pour toujours. Les raisons les plus profondes, les indices les plus graves nous font croire au contraire, nous forcent à penser que la génération suivante, la génération qui vient après celle qui vient immédiatement après nous, et qui bientôt sera la génération de nos enfants, va être enfin une génération mystique. Cette race a trop de sang dans les veines pour demeurer l'espace de plus d'une génération dans les cendres et dans les moisissures de la critique. Elle est trop vivante pour ne pas se réintégrer, au bout d'une génération, dans l'organique.

Tout fait croire que les deux mystiques vont refleurir à la fois, la républicaine et la chrétienne. —

Nous tournant donc vers les jeunes gens, — nous ne pouvons que leur dire : Prenez garde. Vous nous traitez de vieilles bêtes. C'est bien. Mais prenez garde. Quand vous parlez à la légère, quand vous traitez légèrement, si légèrement la

this people no longer believes in the Republic and that it no longer believes in God; that it no longer wishes to lead the Republican life and that it no longer wishes to lead the Christian life. It is fed up. One might almost say that it will no longer believe in idols and that it will no longer believe in the real God. The same disbelief, a single disbelief reaches idols and God, at the same time reaches the false gods and the real God, the gods of antiquity, the new God, the old gods and the God of Christians. A same sterility petrifies the city and Christianity. The political city and the Christian city. The city of men and the city of God. It is properly modern sterility. Let no one rejoice, seeing misfortune come to enemy, adversary, neighbor. For the same misfortune, the same sterility are his.

I do not say that this will always be so. The deepest reasons, the most serious indications lead us to believe the contrary, oblige us to think that the following generation, the generation coming after that which comes immediately after us, and which will soon be the generation of our children, will at last be a generation of mystics. This race has too much blood in its veins to remain in the ashes and mildew of criticism longer than the space of a generation. It is too much alive not to be reinstated at the end of one generation in the organic.

Everything leads one to believe that the two mysticisms— the Republican and the Christian—will flourish anew, together.—

Turning thus to youth,—all we can say to them is: Take care. You call us old fools. That's all right. But take care. When you talk lightly, when you treat the Republic lightly, so lightly, you risk not only being unfair,—you risk being

République, vous ne risquez pas seulement d'être injustes, —
vous risquez d'être sots. — Vous oubliez, vous méconnaissez
qu'il y a eu une mystique républicaine; et de l'oublier et de
la méconnaître ne fera pas qu'elle n'ait pas été. Des hommes
sont morts pour la liberté comme des hommes sont morts pour
la foi. Ces élections aujourd'hui vous paraissent une formalité grotesque, universellement menteuse, truquée de
toutes parts. Et vous avez le droit de le dire. Mais des hommes
ont vécu, des hommes sans nombre, des héros, des martyrs,
et je dirai des saints, — et quand je dis des saints je sais peut-
être ce que je dis, — des hommes ont vécu sans nombre,
héroïquement, saintement, des hommes ont souffert, des
hommes sont morts, tout un peuple a vécu pour que le dernier
des imbéciles aujourd'hui ait le droit d'accomplir cette formalité truquée. Ce fut un terrible, un laborieux, un redoutable enfantement. Ce ne fut pas toujours du dernier grotesque.
Et des peuples autour de nous, des peuples entiers, des races
travaillent du même enfantement douloureux, travaillent et
luttent pour obtenir cette formalité dérisoire. Ces élections
sont dérisoires. Mais il y a eu un temps, un temps héroïque
où les malades et les mourants se faisaient porter dans des
chaises pour aller déposer leur bulletin dans l'urne. Déposer
son bulletin dans l'urne, cette expression vous paraît aujourd'hui du dernier grotesque. Elle a été préparée par un
siècle d'héroïsme. Non pas d'héroïsme à la manque, d'un
héroïsme à la littéraire. Par un siècle du plus incontestable,
du plus authentique héroïsme. —

Ces élections sont dérisoires. Mais l'héroïsme et la sainteté
avec lesquels, moyennant lesquels on obtient des résultats dérisoires, temporellement dérisoires, c'est tout ce qu'il y a de
plus grand, de plus sacré au monde. C'est tout ce qu'il y a

stupid.—You forget, you disregard the fact that there has been a republican mysticism. And to forget and disregard it does not wipe out the fact that it did exist. Men have died for liberty as men have died for faith. Today, these elections seem to you a grotesque formality, universally mendacious, faked on all sides. And you have the right to say so. But men have lived, men without number, heroes, martyrs, and I might say saints,—and when I say saints perhaps I know what I say,—men without number have lived, heroic, saintly lives, men have suffered, men have died, a whole people has lived that the greatest of imbeciles today might have the right to accomplish this faked formality. It was a terrible, a laborious, a dreadful childbirth. It was not always supremely ridiculous. And around us peoples, entire peoples, races travail in the same painful childbirth; travail and struggle to obtain this derisive formality. These elections are derisive. But there was a time, a heroic time, when the sick and the dying had themselves carried in chairs to the ballot booths to cast their votes. Today, the casting of one's vote in a ballot booth is an expression appearing supremely ridiculous to you. It has been prepared by a century of heroism. Not a shoddy heroism, nor a drawing-room heroism. It has been prepared by a century of the most unquestionable, the most authentic heroism.—

These elections are derisive. But the heroism and saintliness with which, through which one obtains derisive, temporally derisive results, are all that is greatest and most sacred in the world. They are all that is most beautiful. You reproach us with the temporal degradation of these results, of our results. See for yourselves. See your own results. You are always telling us of the republican degradation. Is not the degradation of mysticism in politics a common law?—

de plus beau. Vous nous reprochez la dégradation temporelle de ces résultats, de nos résultats. Voyez vous-mêmes. Voyez vos propres résultats. Vous nous parlez toujours de la dégradation républicaine. La dégradation de la mystique en politique n'est-elle pas une loi commune. —

Tout commence en mystique et finit en politique. — L'intérêt, la question, l'essentiel est que dans chaque ordre, dans chaque système la mystique ne soit point dévorée par la politique à laquelle elle a donné naissance. —

La politique se moque de la mystique, mais c'est encore la mystique qui nourrit la politique même.

Car les politiques se rattrapent, croient se rattraper en disant qu'au moins ils sont pratiques et que nous ne le sommes pas. Ici même ils se trompent. Et ils trompent. Nous ne leur accorderons pas même cela. Ce sont les mystiques qui sont même pratiques et ce sont les politiques qui ne le sont pas. C'est nous qui sommes pratiques, qui faisons quelque chose, et c'est eux qui ne le sont pas, qui ne font rien. C'est nous qui amassons et c'est eux qui pillent. C'est nous qui bâtissons, c'est nous qui fondons, et c'est eux qui démolissent. C'est nous qui nourrissons et c'est eux qui parasitent. C'est nous qui faisons les œuvres et les hommes, les peuples et les races. Et c'est eux qui ruinent.

LA MYSTIQUE REPUBLICAINE, c'était quand on mourait pour la République, la politique républicaine, c'est à présent qu'on en vit.

Everything begins in mysticism and ends in politics.—The interest, the question, the essential is that in each order, in each system, mysticism be not devoured by the politics to which it gave birth.—

Politics laugh at mysticism, but it is still mysticism which feeds these same politics.

For the politicians get even with us, or think they get even with us by saying that at least they are practical, and that we are not. In this they deceive themselves and they deceive others. We will not grant them even this much. It is the mystics who are practical, and the politicians who are not. We it is who are practical, who do something, and it is they who are not, who do nothing. It is we who accumulate and they who pillage. It is we who build, it is we who lay foundations and they who demolish. It is we who nourish and they who live as parasites. It is we who create works and men, peoples and races. And they it is who ruin.

REPUBLICAN MYSTICISM meant dying for the Republic; republican politics at present mean living on it.

Il est tres frequent dans l'histoire que de très petites compagnies de petites gens de bien réussissent à faire ce qui a été refusé à de grandes compagnies de grands hommes de bien. Et naturellement il est encore beaucoup plus fréquent que de très petites compagnies de petites gens de mal réussissent à faire ce que de très grandes compagnies de criminels n'avaient point obtenu.

Le triomphe des démagogies est passager. Mais les ruines sont éternelles.

L'ordre, et l'ordre seul, fait en définitive la liberté. Le désordre fait la servitude. Les seuls démagogues ont intérêt à essayer de nous faire croire le contraire.

IT HAS HAPPENED very frequently in history that very small companies of small good people have succeeded in achieving what has been refused to great companies of great men of good will. And naturally, it is still more frequent that very small companies of evil small people succeed in achieving what very great companies of criminals have not obtained.

THE TRIUMPH of demagogies is fleeting. But the ruins are eternal.

ORDER, and order alone, conclusively makes freedom. Disorder makes servitude. Demagogues alone have an interest in making us believe the opposite.

LE SOCIALISME ET LE MONDE MODERNE

NOTRE SOCIALISME — n'était nullement antifrançais, nullement antipatriote, nullement antinational. Il était essentiellement et rigoureusement, exactement international. Théoriquement il n'était nullement antinationaliste. Il était exactement internationaliste. Loin d'atténuer, loin d'effacer le peuple, au contraire il l'exaltait, il l'assainissait. Loin d'affaiblir, ou d'atténuer, loin d'effacer la nation, au contraire il l'exaltait, il l'assainissait. Notre thèse était au contraire, et elle est encore, que c'est au contraire la bourgeoisie, le bourgeoisisme, le capitalisme bourgeois, le sabotage capitaliste et bourgeois qui oblitère la nation et le peuple. Il faut bien penser qu'il n'y avait rien de commun entre le socialisme d'alors, notre socialisme, et ce que nous connaissons aujourd'hui sous ce nom. Ici encore la politique a fait son œuvre, et nulle part autant qu'ici la politique n'a défait, dénaturé la mystique. —

Pour le philosophe, pour tout homme philosophant notre socialisme était et n'était pas moins qu'une religion du salut temporel. Et aujourd'hui encore il n'est pas moins que cela. Nous ne cherchions pas moins que le salut temporel de l'hu-

SOCIALISM AND THE
MODERN WORLD

OUR SOCIALISM—was not in the least anti-French, not in the least antipatriotic, not in the least *anti*national. It was essentially and strictly, exactly *inter*national. Theoretically it was not in the least antinationalistic. It was exactly internationalistic. Far from reducing, far from obliterating the people, it on the contrary exalted and purified it. Far from weakening or reducing, far from obliterating the nation, it on the contrary exalted and purified it. Our theory, on the contrary, was, and still is, that contrarily, what obliterates the nation and the people is the bourgeoisie, bourgeois-ism, bourgeois capitalism, capitalistic and bourgeois sabotage. One must indeed think that there was nothing in common between the socialism of those days, our socialism, and that which we know today under that name. Here again, politics have done their work, and nowhere as much as in this case have politics undone, denatured mysticism.—

For the philosopher, for every man who philosophizes, our socialism was, and was no less than a religion of temporal salvation. And even today, it is no less than this. We sought for no less than the temporal salvation of humanity

manité par l'assainissement du monde ouvrier, par l'assainissement du travail et du monde du travail, par la restauration
du travail et de la dignité du travail, par un assainissement,
par une réfection organique, moléculaire du monde du travail, et par lui de tout le monde économique, industriel. —
Par la restauration des mœurs industrielles, par l'assainissement de l'atelier industriel nous n'espérions pas moins, nous
ne cherchions pas moins que le salut temporel de l'humanité.
Ceux-là seuls s'en moqueront qui ne veulent pas voir que le
christianisme même, qui est la religion du salut éternel, est
embourbé dans cette boue, dans la boue des mauvaises mœurs
économiques, industrielles; que lui-même il n'en sortira
point, qu'il ne s'en tirera point à moins d'une révolution
économique, industrielle; qu'enfin il n'y a point de lieu de
perdition mieux fait, mieux aménagé, mieux outillé pour
ainsi dire, qu'il n'y a point d'outil de perdition mieux adapté
que l'atelier moderne.

Et que toutes les difficultés de l'Église viennent de là,
toutes ses difficultés réelles, profondes, populaires : de ce que,
malgré quelques prétendues œuvres ouvrières, sous le masque
de quelques prétendues œuvres ouvrières et de quelques pré-
tendus ouvriers catholiques, de ce que l'atelier lui est fermé,
et de ce qu'elle est fermée à l'atelier; de ce qu'elle est devenue
dans le monde moderne, subissant, elle aussi, une modernisa-
tion, presque uniquement la religion des riches et ainsi qu'elle
n'est plus socialement si je puis dire la communion des fidèles.
Toute la faiblesse, et peut-être faut-il dire la faiblesse crois-
sante de l'Église dans le monde moderne vient non pas comme
on le croit de ce que la Science aurait monté contre la Religion des systèmes soi-disant invincibles, non pas de ce que
la Science aurait découvert, aurait trouvé contre la Religion

by the purification of the working world, by the purification
of work and of the world of work, by the restoration of work
and of the dignity of work, by a purification, by an organic
molecular repair of the working world, and through it of the
whole economic, industrial world.—By the restoration of
industrial morality, by the purification of the industrial work-
room, we hoped for no less, we sought no less than the temporal salvation of humanity. Only those will laugh who do
not wish to realize that Christianity itself, which is the religion of eternal salvation, is stuck in this mire, in the mire
of rotten economic, industrial morality; those who do not
wish to realize that Christianity itself will not emerge from
it, will not be drawn out of it, save through an economic,
industrial revolution; and lastly that there is no place of
perdition better made, better ordered, and better provided
with tools, so to speak; that there is no more fitting tool of
perdition than the modern work-room.

All the difficulties of the Church come from this, all her
real, deep difficulties, all the difficulties with the people
come from the fact that in spite of a few so-called charities
for workmen, under the cloak of a few so-called charities for
workmen and of a few so-called Catholic workmen, the work-
room is closed to the Church and that she is closed to the
work-room. Because she too, undergoing a modernization, has
become in the modern world, almost entirely the religion
of the rich; and thus, if I may say so, she is no longer socially
the communion of the faithful. All the weakness, and perhaps
one should say the growing weakness of the Church in the
modern world, comes from the fact that what remains today
of the Christian world socially, is profoundly lacking in
charity. It, this same weakness of the Church, does not come

des arguments, des raisonnements censément victorieux, mais
de ce que ce qui reste du monde chrétien socialement manque
aujourd'hui profondément de charité. Ce n'est point du
tout le raisonnement qui manque. C'est la charité. Tous ces
raisonnements, tous ces systèmes, tous ces arguments pseudo-
scientifiques ne seraient rien, ne pèseraient pas lourd s'il y
avait une once de charité. Tous ces airs de tête ne porteraient
pas loin si la chrétienté était restée ce qu'elle était, une communion, si le christianisme était resté ce qu'il était, une religion du cœur. C'est une des raisons pour lesquelles les
modernes n'entendent rien au christianisme, au vrai, au réel,
à l'histoire vraie, réelle du christianisme, et à ce que c'était
réellement que la chrétienté. —

Ainsi dans ce monde moderne tout entier tendu à l'argent,
tout à la tension à l'argent, cette tension à l'argent contami-
nant le monde chrétien même lui fait sacrifier sa foi et ses
mœurs au maintien de sa paix économique et sociale.

C'est là proprement ce modernisme du cœur, ce modernisme
de la charité, ce modernisme des mœurs.

Il y a deux sortes de riches: les riches athées, qui, riches,
n'entendent rien à la religion. Ils se sont donc mis à l'histoire
des religions, et ils y excellent, (et d'ailleurs il faut leur faire
cette justice qu'ils ont tout fait pour n'en point faire une histoire de la religion). C'est eux qui ont inventé les sciences
religieuses; et les riches dévots, qui, riches, n'entendent rien
au christianisme. Alors ils le professent.

Tel est, il faut bien voir, il faut bien mesurer, tel est l'ef-
frayant modernisme du monde moderne; l'effrayante, la
misérable efficacité. Il a entamé, réussi à entamer, il a moder-
nisé, entamé la chrétienté. Il a rendu véreux, dans la charité,
dans les mœurs il a rendu véreux le christianisme même. —

—as people think—from the fact that Science has established so-called invincible systems, that Science has discovered, has found arguments and supposedly victorious reasonings against Religion. Arguments are not in the least lacking. It is charity that is lacking. All these reasonings, all these systems, all the pseudo-scientific arguments would be as nothing, would be of little weight, if there were an ounce of charity. All these intellectual attitudes would have short shrift if Christianity had remained what it was, a communion, if Christianity had remained what it was, a religion of the heart. This is one of the reasons why modern people understand nothing of true, real Christianity, of the true, real history of Christianity and what Christendom really was.—

So this modern world, straining entirely after money, all its efforts tending towards money, contaminates the Christian world itself, causes it to sacrifice its faith and its morals to the maintainance of its economic and social peace.

Properly speaking, this is modernism of heart, modernism of charity, modernism of morality.

There are two kinds of rich men: firstly, rich atheists, who, being rich, understand nothing of religion. So they embark upon the history of religions, and there they excel—(and, moreover, to do them justice, they did all in their power not to turn this into a history of religion). They it was who invented religious sciences; secondly, the pious rich men, who, being rich, understand nothing of Christianism. So they profess it.

Such is, it must be well considered, it must be well pondered, such is the frightful modernism of the modern world—its frightful, its wretched efficiency. It has broached, succeeded in broaching, it has modernized, broached Christianity.

L'Eglise n'est rien de ce qu'elle était, et elle est, devenue, tout ce qu'il y a de plus contraire à elle-même, tout ce qu'il y a de plus contraire à son institution. Et elle ne se rouvrira point l'atelier, et elle ne se rouvrira point le peuple à moins que de faire, elle aussi, elle comme tout le monde, à moins que de faire les frais d'une révolution économique, d'une révolution sociale, d'une révolution industrielle, pour dire le mot d'une révolution temporelle pour le salut éternel. Telle est, éternellement, temporellement, le mystérieux assujettissement de l'éternel même au temporel. Telle est proprement l'inscription de l'éternel même dans le temporel. Il faut faire les frais économiques, les frais sociaux, les frais industriels, les frais temporels. Nul ne s'y peut soustraire, non pas même l'éternel, non pas même le spirituel, non pas même la vie intérieure.

LA REVOLUTION sociale sera morale, ou elle ne sera pas.

A LA PLUPART des grands théoriciens socialistes, il a manqué d'être pauvre.

A MOINS d'avoir du génie, un homme riche ne peut pas imaginer ce qu'est la pauvreté.

In charity, in morals, it has undermined Christianity itself.—

The Church is nothing of what she was and she has become all that is most contrary to herself, all that is most contrary to her institution. And she will not reopen the door of the work-room and she will not be open once more to the people, unless she too, she like the rest of the world, unless she too pays the price of an economic revolution—a social revolution, an industrial revolution, in short, a temporal revolution for eternal salvation. Such is, eternally, temporally, the mysterious subjection of the eternal itself to the temporal. Such is properly the inscription of the eternal itself in the temporal. Economic expenses, social expenses, industrial expenses, temporal expenses must be met. Nothing can evade it, not even the eternal, not even the spiritual, not even the inner life.

THE SOCIAL REVOLUTION will be moral, or it will not be.

TO MOST OF THE great socialist theorists poverty was lacking.

SHORT OF GENIUS, a rich man cannot imagine poverty.

L'AVENIR

QUI SOUTIENDRAIT aujourd'hui que le monde moderne est
le dernier monde, le meilleur, qui au contraire soutiendrait qu'il est le plus mauvais; s'il est le meilleur ou le
pire, nous n'en savons rien; les optimistes n'en savent rien;
les pessimistes n'en savent rien; et les autres non plus; qui
avancerait aujourd'hui que l'humanité moderne est la der-
nière humanité, la meilleure, ou la plus mauvaise; les pessimismes aujourd'hui nous paraissent aussi vains que les
optimismes, parce que les pessimismes sont des arrêts comme
les optimismes, et que c'est l'arrêt même qui nous paraît
vain; qui aujourd'hui se flatterait d'arrêter l'humanité, ou
dans le bon, ou dans le mauvais sens, pour une halte de
béatitude, ou pour une halte de damnation; l'idée que nous
recevons au contraire de toutes parts, du progrès et de
l'éclaircissement des sciences concrètes, physiques, chimi-
ques, et surtout naturelles, de la vérification et de la mise à
l'épreuve des sciences historiques mêmes, de l'action de la
vie et de la réalité, c'est cette idée au contraire que la nature,
et que l'humanité, qui est de la nature, ont des ressources
infinies, et pour le bien, et pour le mal, et pour des infinités

THE FUTURE

W̶HO WOULD MAINTAIN TODAY that the modern world is
the last and best of worlds? Who, on the contrary,
would maintain that it is the worst? Whether it is the best or
the worst, we don't know. The optimists don't know. The
pessimists don't know. And the others don't know either.
Who would assert today that modern humanity is the ultimate
humanity, the best or the worst? Pessimism today appears to
us as vain as optimism, because pessimism, like optimism, is
a halt. And it is the halt itself which appears vain to us. Who
today would flatter himself that he has halted humanity in
the right or wrong direction? Stopping it for a halt of beatitude or a halt of damnation? The idea, on the contrary, which
we receive from all sides—from progress and clarification of
concrete sciences, physics, chemistry and particularly from
natural sciences, even from the verification and testing of historical sciences, from the action of life and of reality—the
idea which comes to us from all sides is that nature and humanity (which is of nature), have infinite resources, for good
and for evil, and for the infinities beyond, which infinities

d'au delà qui ne sont peut-être ni du bien ni du mal, étant
autres, et nouvelles, et encore inconnues; c'est cette idée que
nos forces de connaissance ne sont rien auprès de nos forces
de vie et de nos ressources ignorées, nos forces de connaissance étant d'ailleurs nous, et nos forces de vie au contraire
étant plus que nous, que nos connaissances ne sont rien auprès
de la réalité connaissable, et d'autant plus, peut-être, auprès
de la réalité inconnaissable; qu'il reste immensément à
faire; et que nous n'en verrons pas beaucoup de fait; et
qu'après nous jamais peut-être on n'en verra la fin; que le
vieil adage antique, suivant lequel nous ne nous connaissons
pas nous-mêmes, non seulement est demeuré vrai dans les
temps modernes, et sera sans doute vrai pendant un grand
nombre de temps encore, si, même, il ne demeure pas vrai
toujours, mais qu'il reçoit tous les jours de nouvelles et de
plus profondes vérifications, imprévues des anciens, inat-
tendues, nouvelles perpétuellement; que sans doute il en re-
cevra éternellement; que l'avancement que nous croyons voir
se dessiner revient peut-être à n'avancer que dans l'appro-
fondissement de cette formule antique, à lui trouver tous les
jours des sens nouveaux, des sens plus profonds; qu'il reste
immensément à faire, et encore plus immensément à connaître; que tout est immense, le savoir excepté; surtout qu'il
faut s'attendre à tout; que tout arrive; qu'il suffit d'avoir un
bon estomac; que nous sommes devant un spectacle immense
et dont nous ne connaissons que d'éphémères incidents; que
ce spectacle peut nous réserver toutes les surprises; que nous
sommes engagés dans une action immense et dont nous ne
voyons pas le bout; que peut-être elle n'a pas de bout; que
cette action nous réservera toutes les surprises; que tout est
grand, inépuisable; que le monde est vaste; et encore plus le

perhaps are neither good nor evil, being different, new and still unknown. And this idea develops thus: that our forces of knowledge are nothing compared with our vital forces and our hidden resources. Our forces of knowledge moreover are really ourselves, whereas, contrarily, our vital forces are greater than we. That our knowledge is nothing in the light of knowable reality, and all the more so perhaps, in the light of unknowable reality. That an immense amount remains to be done: that we shall not see much of it done. And that after us, perhaps, the end will never be reached. That the time-honored adage of antiquity according to which we do not know ourselves, not only is true in modern times but will doubtless remain true in a great number of future periods. Even if the adage does not remain true for ever, each day it receives new and deeper substantiations, unexpected, perpetually new, and unforeseen by the ancients; doubtless the old adage will have eternally new substantiations. That the improvements which we believe to see taking shape perhaps come back only to the fathoming of the old formula, finding in it daily new meanings, deeper meanings. That there remains an immense amount to do and a still more immense amount to know. That all is immense, except knowledge. And above all, that we must be ready for everything, that anything can happen. That all we need is a good stomach. That we are before an immense spectacle of which we take in only the most ephemeral incidents. That this spectacle may hold in store for us all kinds of surprises. That we are engaged in an immense action the end of which we do not see. That perhaps there is no end. That this action will hold all imaginable surprises for us. That everything is great, inexhaustible. That the world is vast, and vaster still the world of time. That mother

monde du temps; que la mère nature est indéfiniment féconde; que le monde a de la ressource; plus que nous; qu'il
ne faut pas faire les malins; que l'infime partie n'est rien
auprès du tout; que nous ne savons rien, ou autant que rien;
que nous n'avons qu'à travailler modestement; qu'il faut bien
regarder; qu'il faut bien agir; et ne pas croire qu'on sur-
prendra, ni qu'on arrêtera le grand événement.

Qui de nos jours oserait se flatter d'arrêter l'humanité;
fût-ce dans la béatitude; fût-ce dans la consommation de l'histoire; qui ferait la sourde oreille aux avertissements que nous
recevons de toutes parts.

De la réalité nous avons reçu trop de rudes avertissements;
au moment même où j'écris, l'humanité, qui se croyait civili-
sée, au moins quelque peu, est jetée en proie à l'une des
guerres les plus énormes, et les plus écrasantes, qu'elle ait
jamais peut-être soutenues; deux peuples se sont affrontés,
avec un fanatisme de rage dont il ne faut pas dire seulement
qu'il est barbare, qu'il fait un retour à la barbarie, mais dont
il faut avouer ceci, qu'il paraît prouver que l'humanité n'a
rien gagné peut-être, depuis le commencement des cultures,
si vraiment la même ancienne barbarie peut reparaître au
moment qu'on s'y attend le moins, toute pareille, toute ancienne, toute la même, admirablement conservée, seule sin-
cère peut-être, seule naturelle et spontanée sous les perfec-
tionnements superficiels de ces cultures; les arrachements que
l'homme a laissés dans le règne animal, poussant d'étranges
pousses, nous réservent peut-être d'incalculables surprises;
et sans courir au bout du monde, parmi nos Français mêmes,
quels rudes avertissements n'avons-nous pas reçus, et en quelques années; qui prévoyait qu'en pleine France toute la haine
et toute la barbarie des anciennes guerres civiles religieuses

nature is fruitful beyond limits. That the world is resource-
ful, far more so than we. That we must not be too smart. That
an infinitesimal part is nothing compared with the whole.
That we know nothing, or next to nothing. That we have
only to work modestly. That we must look about us carefully.
That we must go on acting and not believe that we will outwit
or halt the great event.

Who of our day would dare to flatter himself that he could
halt humanity, even halting it in beatitude? Even in the con-
summation of history? Who would turn a deaf ear to the
warnings which we receive from all sides?

As for reality, we have received too many rude warnings.
At the moment of writing *, humanity, which believed itself
civilized—at least to some extent—is a prey to one of the
most enormous and crushing wars that it has, perhaps, ever
had to bear. Two peoples confront each other with fanatical
rage, of which one cannot simply say that it is barbarous,
that it is a return to barbarity, but which, one must admit,
seems to prove that humanity has perhaps gained nothing
since the beginning of culture, if indeed the same old barbarity can reappear at a time when it is least expected, just
the same, just as old, admirably preserved; alone sincere,
perhaps alone natural and spontaneous beneath the superficial improvements of these cultures. The roots that man has
left in the animal world bring forth strange shoots. These
may hold in store for us incalculable surprises. And without
running to the other ends of the world, even here among us
Frenchmen, within a few years, how many rude warnings
have we not received? Who could have foreseen that in the
heart of France, in the heart of modern times, all the hatred

* *Russo-Japanese War in 1904.*

en pleine période moderne serait sur le point d'exercer les mêmes anciens ravages; derechef qui prévoyait, qui pouvait prévoir inversement que les mêmes hommes, qui alors combattaient l'injustice d'Etat, seraient exactement les mêmes qui, à peine victorieux, exerceraient pour leur compte cette même injustice; qui pouvait prévoir, et cette irruption de barbarie, et ce retournement de servitude. — Qui pouvait prévoir que de tant de mal il sortirait tant de bien, et de tant de bien, tant de mal; de tant d'indifférence tant de crise, et de tant de crise tant d'indifférence; qui aujourd'hui répondrait de l'humanité, qui répondrait d'un peuple, qui répondrait d'un homme.

Qui répondra de demain.

HOMERE EST NOUVEAU ce matin, et rien n'est peut-être aussi vieux que le journal d'aujourd'hui.

and barbarity of the old religious civil wars were on the brink of exercising the same bygone ravages? * Who foresaw, who could foresee, on the other hand, that the same men who then fought the injustice of State would be exactly the same men who, no sooner victorious, would wield this same injustice for their own account? Who could foresee both this irruption of barbarity and this reversal of servitude?— Who could foresee that from so much evil would come forth so much good, and from so much good, so much evil? From so much indifference such a crisis and from such a crisis so much indifference? Who today could answer for humanity, who could answer for a people, who could answer for a man?

Who will answer for tomorrow?

HOMER IS NEW this morning and perhaps nothing is as old as today's newspaper.

* *Dreyfus Case.*

LES JUIFS

La politique juive

L'inquiétude juive

THE JEWS

Jewish policy

Jewish unrest

LA POLITIQUE JUIVE

IL Y A UNE POLITIQUE JUIVE. Pourquoi le nier. Ce serait le contraire au contraire qui serait suspect. Elle est sotte, comme toutes les politiques. Elle est prétentieuse, comme toutes les politiques. Elle est envahissante, comme toutes les politiques. Elle est inféconde, comme toutes les politiques. Elle fait les affaires d'Israël comme les politiciens républicains font les affaires de la République. Elle est surtout occupée, comme toutes les politiques, à étouffer, à dévorer, à supprimer sa propre mystique, la mystique dont elle est issue. Et elle ne réussit guère qu'à cela. —

La grande majorité des Juifs est comme la grande majorité des (autres) électeurs. Elle craint la guerre. Elle craint le trouble. Elle craint l'inquiétude. Elle craint, elle redoute plus que tout peut-être le simple dérangement. Elle aimerait mieux le silence, une tranquillité basse. Si on pouvait s'arranger moyennant un silence entendu, acheter la paix en livrant le bouc, payer de quelque livraison, de quelque trahison, de quelque bassesse une tranquillité précaire. Livrer le sang innocent, elle sait ce que c'est. En temps de paix elle craint la guerre. Elle a peur des coups. Elle a peur des affaires. Elle est

JEWISH POLICY

THERE IS A JEWISH POLICY. Why deny it? The contrary, on the contrary, would be suspicious. It is stupid, like all policies, pretentious, like all policies, encroaching, like all policies. It is unfruitful, like all policies. The policy performs Israel's business, as republican politicians perform the Republic's business. Like most policies, it is above all busy stifling, devouring and suppressing its own mysticism, the mysticism from which it sprang. And it scarcely succeeds in anything but that.—

The great majority of Jews is like the great majority of (other) voters. It fears war. It fears troublous times. It fears disquietude. And above all else, it fears, it dreads plain disturbance. It would prefer silence, a base tranquillity. If only some agreement could be reached by means of a knowing silence, if only peace could be bought by delivering up a scapegoat, if only precarious quiet could be purchased with surrender, treachery, baseness. This majority knows what it is to deliver up innocent blood. In times of peace, it fears war. It fears blows. It fears publicity. It is forced to the measure of its own greatness. Urged on alone by an active

forcée à sa propre grandeur. Elle n'est conduite à ses grands
destins douloureux que forcée par une poignée de factieux,
une minorité agissante, une bande d'énergumènes et de fana-
tiques, une bande de forcenés, groupés autour de quelques
têtes qui sont très précisément les prophètes d'Israël. Israël a
fourni des prophètes innombrables, des héros, des martyrs,
des guerriers sans nombre. Mais enfin, en temps ordinaire, le
peuple d'Israël est comme tous les peuples, il ne demande qu'à
ne pas entrer dans un temps extraordinaire. Quand il est dans
une période, il est comme tous les peuples, il ne demande qu'à
ne pas entrer dans une époque. Quand il est dans une période,
il ne demande qu'à ne pas entrer dans une crise. Quand il est
dans une bonne plaine, bien grasse, où coulent les ruisseaux
de lait et de miel, il ne demande qu'à ne pas remonter sur la
montagne, cette montagne fût-elle la montagne de Moïse.
Israël a fourni des prophètes innombrables; plus que cela elle
est elle-même prophète, elle est elle-même la race prophé-
tique. Toute entière, en un seul corps, un seul prophète. Mais
enfin elle ne demande que ceci: c'est de ne pas donner matière
aux prophètes à s'exercer. Elle sait ce que ça coûte. Instinc-
tivement, historiquement, organiquement pour ainsi dire elle
sait ce que ça coûte. Sa mémoire, son instinct, son organisme
même, son corps temporel, son histoire, toute sa mémoire le
lui disent. Toute sa mémoire en est pleine. Vingt, quarante,
cinquante siècles d'épreuves le lui disent. Des guerres sans
nombre, des meurtres, des déserts, des prises de villes, des
exils, des guerres étrangères, des guerres civiles, des captivités
sans nombre. Cinquante siècles de misères, quelquefois
dorées. Comme les misères modernes. Cinquante siècles de
détresses, quelquefois anarchistes, quelquefois masquées de
joies, quelquefois masquées, maquillées de voluptés. Cin-

minority, a handful of rebels and insurgents, a band of fanatics and zealots grouped around a few heads which are precisely the prophets of Israel, it is led towards its great and painful destinies. Israel has given the world innumerable prophets, heroes, martyrs and warriors without number. But, after all, in normal times, the people of Israel, like all other peoples, does not wish to enter into extraordinary times. When it belongs to a period, like all other peoples, it does not wish to enter an epoch. When it belongs to a period, it does not wish to step into a crisis. When it lives in a good rich plain, overflowing with milk and honey, it is reluctant to go up into the mountain, even though it be to the mountain of Moses. Israel has supplied prophets without number. What is more, Israel is itself a prophet, is in itself the prophetic race. Wholly, in a single body, a single prophet. In a word, Israel asks one thing only: to avoid giving the prophets grounds for prophecy. She knows the cost of this. Instinctively, historically, organically so to speak, she knows the cost of this. Her memory, her instinct, even her temporal body, her history, all her memory tell her this. Her whole memory is full of this. Twenty, forty, fifty centuries of ordeals tell her this. Wars without number, murders, deserts, captured cities, exiles, foreign wars, civil wars, captivities without number. Fifty centuries of misery, though sometimes the misery be gilded, like modern misery. Fifty centuries of afflictions, sometimes anarchistic, sometimes masked by joys, sometimes masked and disguised into voluptuousness. Fifty centuries perhaps of neurasthenia. Fifty centuries of wounds and scars, of ever painful injuries. The Pyramids and the Champs Elysées, the kings of Egypt and the kings of the Orient, the whip of eunuchs and the Roman lance, the Temple

quante siècles peut-être de neurasthénie. Cinquante siècles de blessures et de cicatrices, des points toujours douloureux, les Pyramides et les Champs Elysées, les rois d'Egypte et les rois d'Orient, le fouet des eunuques et la lance romaine, le Temple détruit et non rebâti, une inexpiable dispersion leur en ont dit le prix pour leur éternité. Ils savent ce que ça coûte, eux, que d'être la voix charnelle et le corps temporel. Ils savent ce que ça coûte que de porter Dieu et ses agents les prophètes. Ses prophètes les prophètes. Alors, obscurément, ils aimeraient mieux qu'on ne recommence pas. Ils ont peur des coups. Ils en ont tant reçu. Ils aimeraient mieux qu'on n'en parle pas. Ils ont tant de fois payé pour eux-mêmes et pour les autres. On peut bien parler d'autre chose. Ils ont tant de fois payé pour tout le monde, pour nous. Si on ne parlait de rien du tout. Si on faisait des affaires, de(s) bonnes affaires. Ne triomphons pas. Ne triomphons pas d'eux. Combien de chré- tiens ont été poussés à coups de lanières dans la voie du salut. C'est partout pareil. Ils ont peur des coups. Toute l'humanité a généralement peur des coups. Au moins avant. Et après. Heureusement elle n'a quelquefois pas peur des coups pen- dant. Les plus merveilleux soldats peut-être du grand Napo- léon, ceux de la fin, ne provenaient-ils pas généralement de bandes de déserteurs et d'insoumis que les gendarmes impé- riaux avaient poussés, menottes aux mains, avaient refoulés comme un troupeau. —

Ils ont tant fui, tant et de telles fuites, qu'ils savent le prix de ne pas fuir. Campés, entrés dans les peuples modernes, ils voudraient tant s'y trouver bien. Toute la politique d'Israël est de ne pas faire de bruit, dans le monde (on en a assez fait), d'acheter la paix par un silence prudent. Sauf quelques écervelés prétentieux, que tout le monde nomme, de se faire

destroyed and not rebuilt, an unatonable dispersion tell them the price of this for all eternity. They know the cost of being the voice of the flesh and the temporal body. They know the cost of bearing God and His agents the prophets. His prophets which are the prophets. Thus, secretly, they would prefer not to start all over again. They fear blows. They have had so many. They would rather not talk about it. They have so often paid for themselves and for others. Surely there are other things to talk about. They have so often paid for the whole world, for us. Supposing one gave up talking about it once and for all. Why not do business, good business. Let us not triumph, let us not triumph over Israel. How many Christians have been driven with whips into the path of salvation. It is always the same everywhere. They fear blows. As a rule all humanity fears blows. At least, before they fall. And after they fall. Fortunately sometimes blows are not feared while they fall. The best among the great Napoleon's wonderful soldiers were perhaps those who fought for him at the end of his career. Yet these soldiers were generally taken from the ranks of deserters and defaulting recruits whom the imperial gendarmes pushed and drove before them in a handcuffed herd.—

Israel has so often fled, so much and in such a manner that she knows the price of not running away. Camped, included among the modern peoples, she would so much desire to find well-being among them. The whole policy of Israel is to make no noise in the world (enough noise has been made), to purchase peace with prudent silence. Apart from a few pretentious scatterbrains, whom everyone knows by name, Israel wishes to be forgotten. She still has so many smarting bruises. But the whole of Israel's mysticism de-

oublier. Tant de meurtrissures lui saignent encore. Mais toute
la mystique d'Israël est qu'Israël poursuive dans le monde sa
retentissante et douloureuse mission. De là des déchirements
incroyables, les plus douloureux antagonismes intérieurs qu'il
y ait eu peut-être entre une mystique et une politique. Peuple
de marchands. Le même peuple de prophètes. Les uns savent
pour les autres ce que c'est que des calamités.

Les uns savent pour les autres ce que c'est que des ruines ;
toujours et toujours des ruines ; un amoncellement de ruines ;
habiter, passer dans un peuple de ruines, dans une ville de
ruines.

Je connais bien ce peuple. Il n'a pas sur la peau un point
qui ne soit pas douloureux, où il n'y ait un ancien bleu, une
ancienne contusion, une douleur sourde, la mémoire d'une
douleur sourde, une cicatrice, une blessure, une meurtrissure
d'Orient ou d'Occident. Ils ont les leurs, et toutes celles des
autres. —

La sagesse est aussi une vertu d'Israël. S'il y a les Prophètes il y a l'Ecclésiaste. Beaucoup disent *à quoi bon*. Les
sages voyaient surtout qu'on allait soulever un tumulte, insti-
tuer un commencement dont on ne verrait peut-être jamais la
fin, dont surtout on ne voyait pas quelle serait la fin. Dans les
familles, dans le secret des familles on traitait communément
de folie cette tentative. Une fois de plus la folie devait l'em-
porter, dans cette race élue de l'inquiétude. Plus tard, bientôt
tous, ou presque tous, marchèrent, parce que quand un
prophète a parlé en Israël, tous le haïssent, tous l'admirent,
tous le suivent. Cinquante siècles d'épée dans les reins les
forcent à marcher.

mands that Israel should pursue its resounding and painful mission throughout the world. Hence extraordinary lacerations, the most painful of inner antagonisms ever known between mysticism and policy. A people of merchants, the same people one of prophets. The ones know for the others the meaning of calamities.

The ones know for the others the meaning of ruins, ever and ever ruins, piles of ruins. What it means to dwell, to pass midst a people in ruins; through a city in ruins.

I know this people well. Not a square inch of its skin that does not smart with pain, that is not full of old bruises, old contusions, dull pain, the memory of dull pain, scars, wounds, lacerations from the East or from the West. This people not only bears its own battle scars but those of all the other races.—

Wisdom is also one of Israel's virtues. Although there be the Prophets, there is Ecclesiastes. Many say, *well what's the good of that?* The wise saw chiefly that an uprising was about to be staged, something begun which might never end; and particularly, no one could tell how it might end. Within families, within the secret heart of families, this attempt was commonly taxed as folly. Once again in this chosen race of unrest, folly was to triumph. Later, all or almost all, fell into stride because when a prophet speaks in Israel, everyone hates him, everyone admires him, everyone follows him. Fifty centuries of prodding in the ribs with a sword makes them all fall into step.

Ils reconnaissent l'épreuve avec un instinct admirable, avec un instinct de cinquante siècles. Ils reconnaissent, ils saluent le coup. C'est encore un coup de Dieu. La ville encore sera prise, le Temple détruit, les femmes emmenées. Une captivité vient, après tant de captivités. De longs convois traîneront dans le désert. Leurs cadavres jalonneront les routes d'Asie. Très bien, ils savent ce que c'est. Ils ceignent leurs reins pour ce nouveau départ. Puisqu'il faut y passer ils y passeront encore. Dieu est dur, mais il est Dieu. Il punit, et il soutient. Il mène. Eux qui ont obéi, impunément, à tant de maîtres extérieurs, temporels, ils saluent enfin le maître de la plus rigoureuse servitude, le Prophète, le maître intérieur.

With admirable instinct, an instinct fifty centuries old,
they recognize the trial. They recognize, they hail the blow.
Another of God's blows. Once more the city will be taken,
the Temple destroyed, the women carried away. After so
many captivities, yet another captivity lies ahead. Long con-
voys will drag through the desert. Their corpses will be land-
marks along the roads of Asia. Well, they know what it's like.
They gird their loins for this new journey. If it has to be, it
will be done once again. God is hard but He is God. He
punishes and He supports. He leads. They who have with
impunity obeyed so many outer, temporal masters, at last
hail the master of the harshest servitude, the Prophet, the
inner master.

L'INQUIETUDE JUIVE

ÊTRE AILLEURS, le grand vice de cette race, la grande vertu secrète; la grande vocation de ce peuple. Une remontée de cinquante siècles ne le mettait point en chemin de fer que ce ne fût quelque caravane de cinquante siècles. Toute traversée pour eux est la traversée du désert. Les maisons les plus confortables, les mieux assises, avec des pierres de taille grosses comme les colonnes du temple, les maisons les plus immobilières, les plus immeubles, les immeubles les plus écrasants ne sont jamais pour eux que la tente dans le désert. Le granit remplaça la tente aux murs de toile. Qu'importe ces pierres de taille plus grosses que les colonnes du temple. Ils sont toujours sur le dos des chameaux. Peuple singulier. Combien de fois n'y ai-je point pensé. Pour qui les plus immobilières maisons ne seront jamais que des tentes. — Peuple pour qui la pierre des maisons sera toujours la toile des tentes. Et pour nous au contraire c'est la toile des tentes qui était déjà, qui sera toujours la pierre de nos maisons. —

C'est faire beaucoup d'honneur au monde moderne, — c'est en méconnaître le virus que de dire: Le monde moderne est une invention, une forgerie, une fabrication, le monde

JEWISH UNREST

To be elsewhere—the great vice of this race, its great
and secret virtue, the great vocation of this people. A
train journey for this people with fifty centuries of caravans
in its memory, means a caravan journey. Any crossing for
them means the crossing of the desert. The most comfortable
houses, the best built from stones as big as the temple pillars,
the most real of real estate, the most overwhelming of apart-
ment houses will never mean any more to them than a tent
in the desert. Granite replaced the tent with walls of canvas.
These stones, bigger than the temple pillars, don't matter.
This people is always on camel back. How many times have
I not thought about this singular people for whom the solid-
est of houses will never be more than tents.—A people for
whom the stones of houses will always be the canvas of tents.
And for us, on the contrary, the canvas of tents was already,
will always be the stone of our houses.—

It is doing the modern world far too much honor,—we disregard its venom by saying: The modern world is an invention, a forgery, a fabrication; the modern world is invented,
has been invented, entirely fabricated by the Jews over and

moderne est inventé, a été inventé, monté, de toutes pièces, par les Juifs sur nous et contre nous. C'est un régime qu'ils ont fait de leurs mains, qu'ils nous imposent, où ils nous dominent, où ils nous gouvernent, où ils nous tyrannisent; où ils sont parfaitement heureux, où nous sommes, où ils nous rendent parfaitement malheureux.

C'est bien mal connaître le monde moderne, que de parler ainsi. C'est lui faire beaucoup d'honneur. C'est le connaître, c'est le voir bien superficiellement. C'est en méconnaître bien gravement, (bien légèrement), le virus, toute la nocivité. C'est bien en méconnaître toute la misère et la détresse. Premièrement le monde moderne est beaucoup moins monté. Il est beaucoup plus une maladie naturelle. Deuxièmement cette maladie naturelle est beaucoup plus grave, beaucoup plus profonde, beaucoup plus universelle.

Nul n'en profite et tout le monde en souffre. Tout le monde en est atteint. Les modernes mêmes en souffrent. Ceux qui s'en vantent, qui s'en glorifient, qui s'en réjouissent, en souffrent. Ceux qui l'aiment le mieux, aiment leur mal. Ceux mêmes que l'on croit qui n'en souffrent pas en souffrent. Ceux qui font les heureux sont aussi malheureux, plus malheureux que les autres, plus malheureux que nous. Dans le monde moderne, tout le monde souffre du mal moderne. Ceux qui font ceux que ça leur profite sont aussi malheureux, plus malheureux que nous. Tout le monde est malheureux dans le monde moderne.

Les Juifs sont plus malheureux que les autres. Loin que le monde moderne les favorise particulièrement, leur soit particulièrement avantageux, leur ait fait un siège de repos, une résidence de quiétude et de privilège, au contraire le monde moderne a ajouté sa dispersion propre moderne, sa dispersion

against us. That this is a regime made by their hands, imposed upon us, a regime which they have imposed on us, where they dominate us, govern us and tyrannize over us, where they are perfectly happy and where we are, where they make us perfectly unhappy.

To talk thus is to know the modern world very badly. It is to honor it far too much. It is to know and to see it very superficially. It is to very gravely (and very frivolously) disregard its venom and its noxiousness. It is to disregard all its destitution and distress. Firstly, the modern world is not properly designed. It is really more of a natural disease. Secondly, this natural disease is far graver, far deeper, far more universal.

No one profits by it and everyone suffers from it. Everyone is smitten by it. The moderns themselves suffer from it. Those who boast of it, who glory in it, who rejoice in it, suffer from it. Those who love it best, love their disease. Those who pretend to be happy are as unhappy, are more unhappy than the others, more unhappy than we. In the modern world everyone suffers from the modern disease. Those who pretend to profit by it are as unhappy, more unhappy than we are. Everyone is unhappy in the modern world.

The Jews are more unhappy than the others. The modern world does not favor them particularly, does not benefit them particularly, has not given them a resting place, a residence of peace and quiet. Far from it. On the contrary, the modern world has added its own dispersion, its inner dispersion to their century-old dispersion, their ethnical dispersion, to their ancient dispersion. The modern world has added its unrest to their unrest. In the modern world they hold cumulative offices. The modern world has added its misery to their

intérieure, à leur dispersion séculaire, à leur dispersion ethni-
que, à leur antique dispersion. Le monde moderne a ajouté son
trouble à leur trouble; dans le monde moderne ils cumulent;
le monde moderne a ajouté sa misère à leur misère, sa détresse
à leur antique détresse; il a ajouté sa mortelle inquiétude, son
inquiétude incurable à la mortelle, à l'inquiétude incurable
de la race, à l'inquiétude propre, à l'antique, à l'éternelle
inquiétude.

Il a ajouté l'inquiétude universelle à l'inquiétude propre. —
Les antisémites ne connaissent point les Juifs. Ils en parlent,
mais ils ne les connaissent point. Ils en souffrent, évidemment
beaucoup, mais ils ne les connaissent point. Les antisémites
riches connaissent peut-être les Juifs riches. Les antisémites
capitalistes connaissent peut-être les Juifs capitalistes. Les
antisémites d'affaires connaissent peut-être les Juifs d'affaires.
Pour la même raison je ne connais guère que des Juifs pauvres
et des Juifs misérables. Il y en a. Il y en a tant que l'on n'en
sait pas le nombre. J'en vois partout.

Il ne sera pas dit qu'un chrétien n'aura pas porté témoignage pour eux. — Depuis vingt ans je les ai éprouvés, nous
nous sommes éprouvés mutuellement. Je les ai trouvés toujours solides au poste, autant que personne, affectueux, solides,
d'une tendresse propre, autant que personne, d'un attachement, d'un dévouement, d'une piété inébranlable, d'une fidélité, à toute épreuve, d'une amitié réellement mystique, d'un
attachement, d'une fidélité inébranlable à la mystique de
l'amitié.

L'argent est tout, domine tout dans le monde moderne à un
tel point, si entièrement, si totalement que la séparation
sociale horizontale des riches et des pauvres est devenue infiniment plus grave, plus coupante, plus absolue si je puis dire

misery, its distress to their old distress. It has added its mortal unrest, its incurable unrest to the mortal, the incurable unrest of the Jewish race. To the unrest proper to the race, to its ancient, eternal unrest.

It has added universal unrest to unrest proper.—

The anti-Semites do not know the Jews. They talk about them but they do not know them. They suffer from them greatly of course, but they do not know them. Perhaps the rich anti-Semites know the rich Jews. Perhaps the capitalistic anti-Semites know the capitalistic Jews. Perhaps anti-Semitic business-men know Jewish business-men. For the same reason, I only know poor Jews and wretched Jews. There are some. There are so many that they cannot be counted. I see them everywhere.

It shall not be said that a Christian has not borne witness in their favor.—For twenty years I have tested them, we have mutually tested one another. I have always found them firm at their posts, as much as anyone could be, affectionate, firm, as purely tender as anyone could be, fond, devoted, of unshaken piety, firmly faithful, offering really mystical friendship, fond, unshakingly faithful to the mysticism of friendship.

Money is everything; it rules everything in the modern world so entirely and to such an extent that the social separation of the rich and the poor along horizontal lines has become infinitely graver, more cutting and more absolute, if I may say so, than the vertical separation between the Jewish race and the Christians. The hardness of the modern world towards the poor, against the poor, has become so entire, so terrifying and altogether so impious towards the ones and the others, against the ones and against the others.

que la séparation verticale de race des juifs et des chrétiens.
La dureté du monde moderne sur les pauvres, contre les
pauvres, est devenue si totale, si effrayante, si impie ensemble
sur les uns et sur les autres, contre les uns et contre les autres.

Dans le monde moderne les connaissances ne se font, ne se
propagent que horizontalement, parmi les riches entre eux, ou
parmi les pauvres entre eux. —

Pauvre je porterai témoignage pour les Juifs pauvres. —
Dans cette galère du monde moderne je les vois qui rament
à leur banc, autant et plus que d'autres, autant et plus que
nous. Autant et plus que nous subissant le sort commun. Dans
cet enfer temporel du monde moderne je les vois comme nous,
autant et plus que nous, trimant comme nous, éprouvés comme
nous. Epuisés comme nous. Surmenés comme nous. Dans les
maladies, dans les fatigues, dans la neurasthénie, dans tous
les surmenages, dans cet enfer temporel j'en connais des cen-
taines, j'en vois des milliers qui aussi difficilement, plus difficilement, plus misérablement que nous gagnent péniblement
leur misérable vie.

Dans cet enfer commun.

Des riches il y aurait beaucoup à dire. Je les connais beaucoup moins. Ce que je puis dire, c'est que depuis vingt ans
j'ai passé par beaucoup de mains. Le seul de mes créanciers
qui se soit conduit avec moi non pas seulement comme un
usurier, mais ce qui est un peu plus, comme un créancier,
comme un usurier de Balzac, le seul de mes créanciers qui
m'ait traité avec une dureté balzacienne, avec la dureté, la
cruauté d'un usurier de Balzac n'était point un Juif. C'était
un Français, j'ai honte à le dire, on a honte à le dire, c'était
hélas un «chrétien», trente fois millionnaire. Que n'aurait-on
pas dit s'il avait été Juif.

In the modern world, acquaintances are made only, spread only, horizontally—the rich among themselves, the poor among themselves.—

Poor myself, I will bear witness in favor of the poor Jews. —In this galley of a modern world I see them rowing at their bench, as hard and harder than the others, as hard and harder than we. They undergo the common lot as much and more than we. In this temporal hell of the modern world I see that they drudge and are tried like us and more than us. Worn out like us. Overworked like us. In these diseases, fatigues, neurasthenias, in all the overwork of this temporal hell, I know hundreds of them, I see thousands of them who painfully earn their wretched livings, as hard, harder, more miserably than we do.

In this common hell.

About the rich there would be much to say. I know far less about them. What I can say is that in twenty years I have gone through many hands. The single one of my creditors who behaved to me not only like a usurer, but what is saying rather more, like a creditor, like one of Balzac's usurers, the single one of my creditors who treated me with Balzacian harshness, with the harshness, the cruelty of one of Balzac's usurers, was not a Jew. He was a Frenchman, I am ashamed to say. One is ashamed to say that he was, alas, a Christian, a millionaire thirty times over. What wouldn't have been said, had he been a Jew?

GUERRE ET PAIX

WAR AND PEACE

War and Peace

Weakness and Cowardice

The Antipatriots

The Roman Soldier

The Rights of Man

GUERRE ET PAIX

JE PRETENDS que la paix n'est valable et que la paix n'est
ferme que si la guerre précédente, après qu'elle fut
devenue inévitable, a été conduite loyale. Or je connais au
moins deux loyautés, et la seconde n'est pas moins indispensable que la première. La première loyauté consiste à traiter
nos adversaires et nos ennemis comme des hommes, à respecter leur personne morale, à respecter dans notre conduite
envers eux les obligations de la loi morale, à garder, au plus
fort du combat et dans toute l'animosité de la lutte, la propreté,
la probité, la justice, la justesse, la loyauté, à rester honnêtes,
à ne pas mentir. Cette première loyauté est surtout morale.
Je la nommerais la loyauté personnelle. Je reconnais une
seconde loyauté, sur laquelle s'est portée beaucoup moins
l'attention des moralistes. Cette seconde loyauté, qui est
mentale autant que morale, consiste à traiter la guerre elle-
même, après qu'elle est devenue inévitable, comme étant la
guerre et non pas comme étant la paix. Tout bêtement elle
consiste à se battre pour de bon, quand on se bat. Elle consiste
à faire la guerre sérieusement, dans son genre, comme on doit
faire sérieusement tout travail, dans son genre. Elle consiste

WAR AND PEACE

I CLAIM THAT PEACE is neither valid nor firm unless the war which preceded it was not only unavoidable but loyally fought. Now I know of at least two loyalties and the second is no less indispensable than the first. The first loyalty consists in treating our adversaries and enemies as men, in respecting their moral persons, in respecting through our behavior towards them the obligations of moral law and, throughout the heat of battle and the animosity of the struggle, in keeping to cleanliness, probity, justice, loyalty, in remaining honest and abstaining from falsehood. This first loyalty is mainly moral. I will call it personal loyalty. I admit a second loyalty on which the attention of moralists centers far less. This second loyalty is mental as well as moral and consists in treating war itself—once war has become inevitable—as war and not as peace. It consists plainly in this: when one fights, to fight in good earnest. It consists in waging war earnestly, according to its own fashion, as all work must be done, earnestly, according to its own fashion. It consists in fighting hand to hand. It consists in not committing the falsehood of waging war as though it were peace, this being a

à se battre corps pour corps. Elle consiste à ne pas commettre
le mensonge qui consiste à faire de la guerre comme si c'était
de la paix, mensonge de moralité, comme tout mensonge,
mensonge aussi de mentalité, comme toute erreur volontaire
de jugement et d'attitude. Je la nomme la loyauté réelle.

Je prétends que la paix n'est ferme, dans son genre, que si
la guerre précédente a été ferme, dans son genre. Ici l'amertume est salubre. Et c'est la tiédeur, la fadeur, la quiétude et
la moiteur des complaisances moisies qui est pernicieuse. —
L'amertume est saine et féconde. Les batailles amères laissent
le champ libre au travail sain.

La tyrannie est toujours mieux organisée que la liberté.

L'histoire ne passe pas où l'on veut. L'histoire passe où
elle veut. Des hommes, des peuples, des promotions, des races
sans nombre auraient fait des sacrifices inouïs pour être
inscrits au livre temporellement éternel. L'histoire passe toujours ailleurs. Et à ceux qui ne voulaient rien elle donne tout.
Ce sont toujours ceux qui ne s'y attendent pas, qui n'y pensent
pas, qui ne savent pas ce que c'est qui sont frôlés, qui sont
touchés, qui sont fauchés de la grande aile. Ce furent ces
bateliers, ces pêcheurs, ces péagers qui furent comme arrachés
au passage, comme entraînés, enlevés d'un coup d'épaule,
comme râflés par le Fils de Dieu.

On n'a pas le droit de trahir les traîtres même. Les
traîtres il faut les combattre, et non pas les trahir.

moral falsehood, like all falsehoods and also a mental falsehood, like all wilful mistakes of judgement and attitude. I
call this real loyalty.

I claim that peace is not firm, after its own fashion, unless
the preceding war has been firm, after its own fashion. Bitterness is healthy here. Lukewarmness, tameness, quietude and
the dampness of mildewed compliances are pernicious.—
Bitterness is healthy and fruitful. Bitter battles leave the field
clear for healthy work.

TYRANNY IS ALWAYS better organized than freedom.

HISTORY DOES NOT go where one would wish. History goes
where it wishes. Innumerable men, peoples, promotions, races
would have made unheard-of sacrifices to be inscribed in
the temporally eternal book. History always passes them by.
And to those who wanted nothing, she gives everything. It is
always those who do not expect, who do not think of it, who
do not know what it is all about, they it is who are grazed,
who are touched, who are mowed down by the great wing.
It was those boatmen, those fishermen, those toll-gatherers
who were waylaid, torn away, swept off, carried up, shoul-
dered up, kidnapped, as it were, by the Son of God.

ONE HAS NOT THE RIGHT to betray even a traitor. Traitors
must be fought and not betrayed.

FAIBLESSE ET LACHETE

Tous les regimes de faiblesse, tous les régimes de capitulation devant l'ennemi sont aussi ceux des plus grands massacres de la population militaire et de la population civile. Rien n'est meurtrier comme la faiblesse et la lâcheté. Rien n'est humain comme la fermeté. — Les régimes de lâcheté sont ceux qui coûtent le plus au monde, et en définitive ce sont ceux qui peuvent finir et les seuls qui finissent réellement dans l'atrocité. Et en outre c'est une atrocité de turpitude. Il n'y a que deux politiques. En temps de guerre les régimes qui ne réduisent pas immédiatement les ennemis de l'intérieur sont inévitablement conduits à massacrer des portions entières et considérables du peuple; ou si l'on veut les régimes qui ne commencent pas par mettre au pas les ennemis de l'intérieur, c'est-à-dire, pour les nommer, quelques misérables intellectuels et politiciens finissent toujours par massacrer le peuple, les régimes qui ne commencent pas par annuler les mauvais bergers finissent toujours par massacrer le troupeau même. —

En temps de guerre il n'y a plus que l'Etat. Et c'est *Vive la Nation.*

En temps de guerre celui qui ne se rend pas est mon homme, quel qu'il soit, d'où qu'il vienne, et quel que soit son parti. Il ne se rend point. C'est tout ce qu'on lui demande. Et celui qui se rend est mon ennemi, quel qu'il soit, d'où qu'il vienne, et quel que soit son parti. Et je le hais d'autant plus, et je le méprise d'autant plus que par les jeux des partis politiques il prétendrait s'apparenter à moi.

ALL REGIMES OF WEAKNESS and capitulation before the enemy are also those which result in the greatest massacres of military and civilian populations. Nothing is as murderous as weakness and cowardice. Nothing is as humane as firmness.—Regimes of cowardice are those which cost the world most and eventually prove those which can end, and the only ones which really do end, in atrocity. Moreover, this is the atrocity of turpitude. There are only two policies. In war times the regimes which do not at once reduce the enemies within the country are unavoidably led to massacre entire and considerable portions of the people. Or, if you like, regimes which do not begin by bringing into line the enemies inside the country, always end by massacring the people. By enemies inside the country I mean a few wretched intellectuals and politicians. And regimes which do not begin by extirpating the bad shepherds always end by butchering the flock itself.—

In war times nothing remains but the State. And this means *long live the Nation.*

In war times, he who does not surrender is a man after my own heart, no matter who he is, no matter whence he comes, no matter what his party. He does not surrender, that is all that is asked of him. And he who surrenders is my enemy, no matter who he is, no matter whence he comes, no matter what his party. And I hate him all the more, I scorn him all the more if, through the play of political parties, he can claim kinship with myself.

LES ANTIPATRIOTES

Nos antipatriotes éprouveront que dans le système char-
nel et même dans un système mystique temporel, dans
tout système temporel, il faut un corps, une chair temporelle
qui soit le soutien, matériel, qui se fasse le support, la matière
d'une idée. C'est très exactement, dans l'ordre politique et
social, dans l'ordre historique, le problème de la relation du
corps à l'esprit. Comme dans la création naturelle nous ne
connaissons pas naturellement d'esprit qui n'ait le support
de quelque corps (généralement quelque mémoire qui n'ait
le support de quelque matière), qui ne soit incorporé de
quelque sorte, et incarné (et c'est même la seule définition
peut-être un peu sérieuse que l'on puisse donner de la création naturelle) de même nous ne connaissons pas naturellement d'idée, d'esprit politique ou social, — j'oserai dire,
religieux, — qui ait pu apparaître sans un certain *corpus*,
sans un appui, sans un soutien, sans un mécanisme, sans un
support de peuple, sans une matière, en un mot sans une
patrie. Au sage il a fallu la cité hellénique; au prophète il a
fallu la race et le peuple d'Israël; au saint il a fallu le peuple
chrétien. Et certains peuples de l'Occident, au moins pour

THE ANTIPATRIOTS

O UR ANTIPATRIOTS will experience in the carnal and even
in the mystical temporal system, in any temporal system, that a body, a temporal flesh is needed as a material
support, to become the support, the matter of an idea. This,
precisely in the very political and social order, in the historical order, is the problem of relations between body and spirit.
As, in natural creation we naturally do not know spirit without bodily support (as a rule, there is no memory not supported by some matter), we do not know spirit which is not,
to a certain extent, incorporate and incarnate (and this, in
fact, is possibly the only rather serious definition which can
be given of natural creation). Again, we naturally cannot
conceive of an idea, pertaining to the political or social
spirit, I would even dare to say the religious spirit—which
has been able to appear without a certain *corpus*—without a
prop or stay, without a mechanism, without the support of a
people, without matter—in a word, without a fatherland.
The philosopher had to have the Greek city. The prophet had
to have the race and people of Israel. The saint had to have
the Christian people and certain Occidental peoples, at least

commencer. Et il n'est pas jusqu'à cette sorte de préformation temporelle de l'Empire romain dans et pour l'avènement du christianisme, si importante, qui charnelle, corporelle, matérielle, ne nous paraisse en effet d'une importance comme excessive, très vraiment inquiétante. Nos positivistes apprendront la métaphysique comme nos pacifistes apprendront la guerre. Nos positivistes apprendront a métaphysique à coups de fusils. Mutuels. Je veux dire qu'ils donneront et qu'ils recevront. Ils apprendront même la psychologie. Ils apprendront la relation du corps d'un peuple à un esprit d'un peuple. Nos antimilitaristes apprendront la guerre, et la feront très bien. Nos antipatriotes apprendront le prix d'une patrie charnelle, d'une cité, d'une race, d'une communion même charnelle, et ce que vaut, pour y appuyer une Révolution, un peu de terre.

to make a start. And even the kind of temporal preformation of the Roman Empire in and for the advent of Christianity which was of such carnal, corporal, material importance, indeed appears to us as even of excessive and most disquieting importance. Our positivists will learn metaphysics as our pacifists will learn war. Our positivists will learn metaphysics by the firing of rifles. And that mutually, for I mean firing and being fired at. They will learn even psychology. They will learn the relation between a people's body and a people's spirit. Our antimilitarists will learn war and they will wage it very well. Our antipatriots will learn the price of a carnal fatherland, of a city, of a race, of a communion— be it a communion of the flesh—and, to support a revolution, the value of a parcel of earth.

LE SOLDAT ROMAIN

L'ARMATURE MILITAIRE est le berceau temporel où les mœurs et les lois et les arts et la religion même et le langage et la race peuvent ensuite, mais ensuite seulement, et alors seulement, se coucher pour grandir. — Le soldat mesure la quantité de terre où on parle une langue, où règnent des mœurs, un esprit, une âme, un culte, une race. —

Il faut aller plus loin. Non seulement c'est le soldat romain qui a porté la voûte romaine, — mais il a porté le temple, — il a mesuré la terre pour les deux seuls grands héritages de l'homme; pour la philosophie et pour la foi; pour la sagesse et pour la foi; pour le monde antique et pour le monde chrétien; pour Platon et pour les prophètes; pour la pensée et pour la foi; pour l'idée et pour Dieu.

Le soldat romain a mesuré la terre et séparé les peuples en deux. Il y a ceux qui en ont été et ceux qui n'en ont pas été et éternellement il y aura ceux qui en ont été et ceux qui n'en ont pas été. —

Il n'a pas fait seulement le monde romain et le monde latin. En dedans ils portaient le monde grec. C'est-à-dire la première moitié du monde antique. Et la pensée antique ne se fût point insérée dans le monde et elle n'eût point commandé la pensée de tout le monde si le soldat romain n'eût point procédé à cette insertion temporelle, si le soldat romain

THE ROMAN SOLDIER

THE MILITARY scaffolding is the temporal cradle where customs, laws, arts, religion even, tongue and race can, once it is ensured and then only, lie down to grow.—

The soldier measures the space of land where a tongue is spoken, where reign customs, a spirit, a soul, a religion, a race.—

We must go further. The Roman soldier not only supported the Roman arch, but the temple also;—he measured the earth for the two sole great inheritances of man; for philosophy and for faith; for wisdom and for faith; for the old world and the Christian world; for Plato and for the Prophets; for thought and for faith; for idea and for God.

The Roman soldier measured the earth and divided its peoples in two. There are those that belonged, and those that did not, and there will eternally be those that belonged, and those that did not.—

He made not only the Roman and Latin worlds. Within, they bore the Greek world. That is, the first half of the ancient world. And ancient thought would not have been inserted into the world and it would not have commanded the thought of the whole world if the Roman soldier had not proceeded to this temporal insertion, if the Roman soldier had not measured the earth, if the Roman world had not proceeded to make this sort of graft, unique in the world—unique in the

n'eût point mesuré la terre, si le monde romain n'eût point procédé à cette sorte de greffe unique au monde, unique dans l'histoire du monde, où Rome fournit la force et les Grecs la pensée, où Rome fournit l'ordre et les Grecs l'invention, où Rome fournit l'empire et les Grecs l'idée, où Rome fournit la terre et les Grecs le point de source, où Rome fournit la matière et le temporel et les Grecs le spirituel et même ce que l'on pourrait nommer la matière spirituelle. Où Rome fournit le sauvageon, et les Grecs le point de culture.

Il faut aller plus loin. C'est un des plus grands mystères mystiques, — on me permettra de joindre ces deux mots, — que la nécessité de Rome dans la destination temporelle de Dieu. Il fallait qu'il y eût la voûte et l'empire et la tortue et le *vallum* pour que le monde chrétien prît cette forme temporelle qu'il devait recevoir et garder. — Il fallut le préfet pour qu'il y eût l'évêque. C'est certainement un des plus grands mystères du monde, et c'en est peut-être le plus grand, que cette inquiétante, que cette mystérieuse place laissée au temporel dans le mécanisme total et ainsi dans le gouvernement, dans le sort du spirituel. Quelle ne faut-il pas que soit cette importance, quelle ne faut-il pas que soit cette gravité pour que la plus grande création spirituelle qu'il y ait jamais eu dans le monde ait été ainsi versée dans un moule temporel que le soldat avait préalablement établi.

Non seulement Virgile, non seulement le monde grec ont été versés dans cette figure de la terre que le soldat romain avait préalablement établie, mais les apôtres mêmes y ont été versés. —

Tout a été forcé de se revêtir du manteau romain. Et ainsi en un certain sens tout a été forcé de se revêtir du manteau militaire.

history of the world, where Rome furnished strength and the Greeks thought, where Rome furnished order and the Greeks invention, where Rome furnished the empire and the Greeks the idea, where Rome furnished land and the Greeks the initial spring, where Rome furnished matter and the temporal order and the Greeks the spiritual order and what could even be called spiritual matter, where Rome furnished the wilding and the Greeks the starting point of culture.

We must go further. One of the greatest of mystical mysteries—I must be allowed to join these two words—is the necessity of Rome in the temporal purpose of God. In order that the Christian world might assume that temporal form which it was to receive and keep, the arch and empire, the *vallum* * and tortoise,** had to exist.—There had to be a prefect in order to have a bishop. Certainly one of the greatest mysteries in the world, and perhaps the greatest, is the disquieting, the mysterious place reserved for the temporal in the total mechanism and thus, in the government, in the destiny of the spiritual. How great, how grave this importance must be for the greatest spiritual creation that ever was in this world to have been thus poured into a temporal mould previously established by the soldier.

Not only Virgil, not only the Greek world have been poured into the earthen figure previously established by the Roman soldier, but the Apostles themselves were poured **therein.**—

Everything has been obliged to don the Roman cloak. And thus, in a certain sense, everything has been obliged to don the military cloak.

---

* *Vallum: Earthwork which served as a visible delimitation of the civil frontier of Rome.*

** *Tortoise: Testudo, a device of locking together the Roman legionaries' shields to form a sort of shell, under which they advanced to the attack.*

LES DROITS DE L'HOMME

CELUI QUI fait jouer la prière et le sacrement pour se dispenser de travailler et d'agir, c'est-à-dire en temps de guerre pour se dispenser de se battre, rompt l'ordre de Dieu même et le commandement le plus antique, et il rompt par trois monstrueuses ruptures, car il retourne contre la loi de travail, contre le commandement de travail la prière et le sacrement qui je pense ne nous ont pas été donnés pour cela; pour nous encourager, pour nous préparer à désobéir. — Autant il est permis, autant il est beau, autant il est profond de demander par la prière, de demander dans la prière le couronnement de fortune et ce sort des batailles qui ne réside que dans l'événement, autant il est stupide, et il est de désobéissance de vouloir que le bon Dieu travaille à notre place, et d'avoir le toupet de le lui demander. Demander la victoire et n'avoir pas envie de se battre, je trouve que c'est mal élevé. —

C'est un système fort connu, et que l'on a toujours nommé le système de la paix à tout prix. C'est une échelle des valeurs où l'honneur est moins cher que la vie. —

THE RIGHTS OF MAN

THE MAN WHO USES prayer and sacrament as an excuse to refrain from work and action, that is, in war times to refrain from fighting, goes against the order of God Himself and against the most ancient commandment, and he breaks it by three monstrous breaks; for in doing so he turns prayer and sacrament against the law of work, against the commandment of work. Prayer and sacrament were not given us, I think, to encourage, to prepare us to disobedience.—Whereas it is permissible, beautiful and deep to ask by prayer, to ask in prayer for the coronation of fortune and that fate of battles which does not reside in the event, it is stupid and disobedient to wish the Good Lord to work in our place and to have the nerve to ask this of Him. To ask for victory and not to feel like fighting, I consider that ill-bred.—

This is a well-known system which has always been called the system of peace at any price. This is a scale of values where honor is cheaper than life.—

C'est un pacifisme à tout prix, un système de la paix, à tout prix. J'y consens, mais ce qu'il y a de saugrenu, ce qu'il y a d'intenable, c'est de mettre un pacifisme, et si je puis dire un pacifisme intégral, sous l'égide, et sous l'invocation de la Déclaration des Droits de l'Homme. — La Déclaration des Droits de l'Homme a justement été faite, elle a été justement introduite dans le monde pour expliquer que le droit passait avant tout, et par conséquent notamment avant la paix. —

Quelle folie, que de vouloir lier à la Déclaration des Droits de l'Homme une Déclaration de Paix. Comme si une Déclaration de Justice n'était pas en elle-même et instantanément une Déclaration de guerre. Il n'y a qu'une Dame dans le monde qui ait fait faire plus de guerres que l'injustice: et c'est la justice. —

Je ne suis pas venu apporter la paix mais la guerre. —

Non seulement la justice mais la charité même est pleine de guerre. Ou plutôt il faut dire: Sans aller même jusqu'à la justice, jusqu'aux revendications, jusqu'aux réparations, jusqu'aux exigences du droit et de la rigoureuse justice, dès la charité même nous savons bien que la charité est source de guerre. Tel est précisément le sort temporel. Tel est le sort de l'homme et du monde. —

L'idée de la paix à tout prix, — l'idée centrale du pacifisme, c'est que la paix est un absolu, c'est que la paix est même le premier des absolus, c'est que la paix a un prix unique à ce point que mieux vaut une paix dans l'injustice qu'une guerre pour la justice. C'est diamétralement le contraire du système des Droits de l'Homme où mieux vaut une guerre pour la justice qu'une paix dans l'injustice.

This is pacifism at any price, a system of peace at any price. I consent to this, but what is absurd and untenable is to place pacifism and if I may say so, complete pacifism under the shield and under the invocation of the Declaration of the Rights of Man.—The Declaration of the Rights of Man was precisely made, precisely introduced into the world to explain that right passed before everything and consequently, before peace.—

It is madness to wish to bind a Declaration of Peace to the Declaration of the Rights of Man. As though a Declaration of Justice were not in itself and instantaneously a declaration of war. There is only one Lady in the world who has caused more wars than injustice: and that is justice.—

I come not to send peace, but a sword.—

Not only justice but charity itself is full of war. Or rather, it should be said: Without going as far as justice even, as far as claims, as far as reparations, as far as exactions of right and of strict justice, beginning with charity itself we know very well that charity is a source of war. Precisely such is the temporal lot. Such is the lot of man and of the world.—

The idea of peace at any price,—the central idea of pacifism, is that peace is an absolute, that peace is even the first of absolutes, that peace has a price unique to this point that a peace in injustice is better than a war for justice. This is the diametrical opposite of the system of the Rights of Man where it is better to have a war for justice than peace in injustice.

LA VIE CHRETIENNE

Charité

La Guerre Sainte

Pécheurs et Saints

De la Sainteté

THE CHRISTIAN LIFE

Charity

The Holy War

Sinners and Saints

Of Sanctity

CHARITE

JE NE VEUX RIEN savoir d'une charité chrétienne qui serait une capitulation constante (du spirituel) devant les puissances temporelles. Je ne veux rien savoir d'une charité chrétienne qui serait une capitulation constante devant les princes, et les riches, et les puissances d'argent. Je ne veux rien savoir d'une charité chrétienne qui serait un constant abandonnement du pauvre et de l'opprimé. Je ne reconnais qu'une charité chrétienne, et c'est celle qui procède directement de Jésus: c'est la constante communion, et spirituelle, et temporelle, avec le pauvre, avec le faible, avec l'opprimé.

DES MILLIERS DE CREANCIERS répètent machinalement les effrayantes paroles: *Et dimitte nobis debita nostra, sicut et nos dimittimus debitoribus nostris.* Qu'un seul tout à coup, soudainement éclairé, les prenne au sérieux, ces paroles, les laisse comme lui entrer dedans, c'est instantanément la plus grande révolution qu'il puisse y avoir.

IL NE SUFFIT malheureusement pas d'être catholique. Il faut encore travailler dans le temporel, si on veut arracher l'avenir aux tyrannies temporelles.

C H A R I T Y

I WILL HAVE NONE OF A Christian charity which would
mean the constant capitulation (of the spiritual) before
temporal powers. I will have none of a Christian charity
which would be a constant capitulation before princes and
rich men, before the powers of money. I will have none of a
Christian charity which would be a constant abandon of the
poor and the oppressed. I recognize one Christian charity
only and it is that which comes directly from Jesus: it is the
spiritual, temporal and constant communion with the poor,
the weak and the oppressed.

THOUSANDS OF CREDITORS mechanically repeat the terrifying words: *Et dimitte nobis debita nostra, sicut et nos dimit-*
timus debitoribus nostris. If a single one among them all,
suddenly enlightened, took these words seriously, allowed
them to enter his being, instantly the greatest possible revolution would take place.

UNFORTUNATELY, it is not enough to be a Catholic. One
must still work in the temporal if one wishes to tear the
future from temporal tyrannies.

LA GUERRE SAINTE

QUAND ON PARLE des âges de foi si l'on veut dire que pendant des siècles, qui étaient des siècles de chrétienté, qui étaient des siècles de la loi d'amour, qui étaient des siècles du règne de la grâce, *anni Domini, anni gratiae Domini,* la foi, la créance était commune, était pour ainsi dire et littéralement publique, était dans le sang et dans les veines communes, dans le peuple, allait de soi, était pour ainsi dire de droit commun, recevait non pas seulement un assentiment mais une célébration publique, solennelle, officielle, et qu'aujourd'hui il n'en est plus de même on a raison. On a historiquement raison. On ne fait que constater, qu'enregistrer un fait historique. Mais ici encore il ne faut l'enregistrer qu'avec la plus extrême attention, il ne faut le manier qu'avec la circonspection la plus extrême.

Il est d'abord permis de se demander si nos fidélités modernes, forcément devenues privées, je veux dire non publiques en ce sens qu'elles ne reçoivent généralement plus la célébration publique, la célébration du peuple et de l'Etat, non solennelles, non officielles, c'est une question de savoir — si nos fidélités, si nos créances modernes, c'est-à-dire chrétiennes

THE HOLY WAR

IF WHILE SPEAKING OF the ages of faith one means that
during the centuries which were centuries of Christianity,
centuries ruled by the law of love, centuries reigned over by
grace, *anni Domini, anni gratiae Domini,* that faith and belief were common, were, so to speak and literally, public,
blended in common with the blood that flowed through the
people's veins, one would be right. If while so speaking one
means that this was an understood thing, so to say of common law, receiving not only assent but a public, solemn,
official celebration, one would be right. And while saying
that today things are no longer so, once more one would be
right. One would be historically right. One would merely be
stating and recording a historical fact. But here again it must
be recorded only with the utmost attention, be handled with
the utmost circumspection.

Our modern faiths have perforce become private, I mean
non-public in the sense that they generally no longer receive
public celebration, the celebration of people and State, and
thus have become non-solemn, non-official. It is therefore permissible first to ask oneself if our modern faiths and beliefs,

baignant dans le monde moderne, traversant intactes le monde moderne, l'âge moderne, les siècles modernes, les deux et les plusieurs siècles intellectualistes n'en reçoivent pas une singulière beauté, une beauté non encore obtenue, et une singulière grandeur aux yeux de Dieu. C'est une question éternelle que de savoir si nos saintetés modernes, c'est-à-dire nos saintetés chrétiennes plongeant dans le monde moderne, dans cette *vastatio*, dans cet abîme d'incrédulité, d'incréance, d'infidélité du monde moderne, isolées comme des phares qu'assaillerait en vain une mer depuis bientôt trois siècles démontée ne sont pas, ne seraient pas les plus agréables aux yeux de Dieu. — Qu'assaillis de toutes parts, éprouvés de toutes parts, nullement ébranlés nos constances modernes, nos fidélités modernes, nos créances modernes, chronologiquement modernes, isolées dans ce monde moderne, battues dans tout un monde, inlassablement assaillies, infatigablement battues, inépuisablement battues des flots et des tempêtes, toujours debout, seules dans tout un monde, debout dans toute une mer inépuisablement démontée, seules dans toute une mer, intactes, entières, jamais, nullement ébranlées, jamais, nullement ébréchées, jamais, nullement entamées, finissent par faire, par constituer, par élever un beau monument à la face de Dieu.

A la gloire de Dieu.

Et surtout et j'y insiste un monument que l'on n'avait jamais vu. Que notre situation soit nouvelle, que notre combat soit nouveau, ce n'est peut-être pas à nous de le dire, mais enfin qui ne voit que notre situation est nouvelle, que notre combat est nouveau. Que cette Eglise moderne, que cette chrétienté moderne, — chrétienne baignant dans le monde moderne, chrétienne traversant le monde moderne, la période moderne, a une sorte de grande beauté tragique propre, presque une

that is to say Christian ones steeped in the modern world,
moving intact across the modern world, the modern age,
the modern centuries, both of them and the several intellec-
tualistic centuries, have not received from these a singular
beauty, a beauty so far unacquired, and a singular grandeur
in the eyes of God. The question of knowing whether our
modern sanctities, that is to say, our Christian sanctities,
those modern sanctities, plunged in the modern world, in this
vastatio, in this abyss of incredulity, of disbelief and unfaith-
fulness of the modern world, isolated like beacons vainly
assailed during well-nigh three centuries of raging furious
sea, are not, will not be, the most pleasing in the eyes of God
is an everlasting question.—Assailed on all sides, tried on
all sides and by no means shaken, our modern beliefs, chron-
ologically modern, isolated in this modern world, knocked
about by a whole world, untiringly assailed, indefatigably
beaten, inexhaustibly beaten by waves and tempests, these
beliefs end by making, by constituting, by erecting a splendid
monument to the presence of God. Forever standing, alone
in a whole world, standing in a whole sea inexhaustibly
stormy, alone in the entire sea, intact, whole, never in any
way shaken, never in any way breached, never in any way
broached, our modern loyalties, faiths and beliefs end by
making, constituting and erecting a splendid monument to
the presence of God.

To the glory of God.

And above all, I insist upon it, this is a monument such
as has never been seen. Perhaps it is not for us to say that
our situation is new, that our struggle is new. But, after all,
who cannot see that our situation is new, that our struggle
is new? That this modern Church, that this modern Christi-

grande beauté non pas de veuve mais de femme qui seule garde une Forteresse — intacte pour le Seigneur et pour le Maître, pour l'Epoux. —

Miles Christi, tout chrétien est aujourd'hui un soldat; le soldat du Christ. Il n'y a plus de chrétien tranquille. Ces Croisades que nos pères allaient chercher jusque sur les terres des Infidèles, *non solum in terras Infidelium, sed, ut ita dicam, in terras ipsas infideles,* ce sont elles aujourd'hui qui nous ont rejoints au contraire, — et nous les avons à domicile. Nos fidélités sont des citadelles. — Le moindre de nous est un soldat. Le moindre de nous est littéralement un croisé. Nos pères comme un flot de peuple, comme un flot d'armée envahissaient des continents infidèles. A présent au contraire c'est le flot d'infidélité au contraire qui tient la mer, qui tient la haute mer et qui incessamment nous assaille de toutes parts. Toutes nos maisons sont des forteresses *in periculo maris,* au péril de la mer. La guerre sainte est partout. Elle est toujours. —

Nous sommes tous aujourd'hui placés à la brèche. Nous sommes tous à la frontière. La frontière est partout.

anity,—Christian and steeped in the modern world, Christian and moving across the modern world, the modern period,— has a sort of great tragic beauty of its own, almost the great beauty not of a widow but of a woman who alone holds a Fortress—intact for the Lord and Master, for the Spouse.—

Miles Christi, today every Christian is a soldier; the soldier of Christ. There are no more quiescent Christians. Those Crusades which our fathers waged as far as the lands of the Infidels, *non solum in terras Infidelium, sed, ut ita dicam, in terras ipsas infideles,* today, those Crusades have come to us and we have them at home. Our faiths are citadels.— The least among us is a soldier. The least among us is liter- ally a crusader. Our fathers like a flood of people, like a flood of armies, invaded the infidel continents. Nowadays, on the contrary, it is a flood of infidelity that holds the seas, the high seas, and that continuously assails us from all sides. All our houses are fortresses, *in periculo maris,* in peril of the sea. The holy war is everywhere. It is ever being waged.—

All of us stand on the breach today. We are all stationed at the frontier. The frontier is everywhere.

PÉCHEURS ET SAINTS

LA LIAISON des pécheurs aux saints est une liaison de communion. Ce qui fait que l'on est ou que l'on n'est pas
de chrétienté, ce n'est pas, ce n'est aucunement, — (on
m'entend bien), — que l'on est plus ou moins pécheur. C'est
une toute autre question, c'est un infiniment autre débat. La
discrimination est toute autre. Le pécheur est de chrétienté.
Le pécheur peut faire la meilleure prière. Nul n'est peut-être
aussi profondément de chrétienté que Villon. Et nulle prière,
je dis nulle prière de saint, ne dépasse la Ballade qu'il fit à
la requête de sa mère pour prier Notre Dame. Le pécheur est
partie intégrante, pièce intégrante du mécanisme de chrétienté. Le pécheur est au cœur même de chrétienté.

La question d'être ou de ne pas être pécheur, ou plutôt
la question d'être plus ou moins pécheur, — (tout le monde
est pécheur), — n'a absolument rien de commun, n'a pour
ainsi dire absolument aucun point de contact avec la question
d'être plus ou moins chrétien, et d'être chrétien ou de ne
l'être pas. C'est une toute autre question, un débat infiniment
autre. Et c'est un des contresens les plus graves que l'on
puisse commettre en matière de chrétienté que de les con-

SINNERS AND SAINTS

THE BOND BETWEEN sinners and saints is a bond of communion. The fact that one belongs or does not belong
to Christianity does not in the least mean—(if you understand
me),—that the one is more or less a sinner. This is quite another question, a debate of an infinitely different nature. The
discrimination is of quite another nature. The sinner belongs
to Christianity. A sinner can make the best prayer. No one
perhaps is so deeply a Christian as Villon. And no prayer,
I say no prayer made by a saint, surpasses the ballad which
he wrote at his mother's request to entreat Our Lady. The
sinner is an integral portion, an integral part of the Christian
mechanism. The sinner lies at the very heart of Christianity.

The question of being or of not being a sinner, or rather,
of being more or less of a sinner,—(everyone is a sinner)—
has absolutely nothing in common, has so to speak, absolutely
no point of contact with the question of being more or less of
a Christian and of being a Christian or of not being one.
This is quite another question, quite another debate. And
one of the most serious misinterpretations that could be committed in the matter of Christianity would be that which

fondre, un de ceux qui marquent le mieux, et le plus instantanément, que l'on n'y entend pas, que l'on n'y est pas, que
l'on ne sait pas de quoi on parle. Que l'on y est totalement in-
compétent. Que l'on y est étranger. Nul au contraire n'est
moins étranger, nul n'est aussi compétent que Villon en
matière de chrétienté. Nul n'est aussi compétent que le pécheur
en matière de chrétienté. Nul, si ce n'est le saint. Et en principe c'est le même homme. —

Le pécheur et le saint sont deux parties on peut le dire
également intégrantes, deux pièces également intégrantes du
mécanisme de chrétienté. Ils sont l'un et l'autre ensemble deux
pièces également indispensables l'une à l'autre, deux pièces
mutuellement complémentaires. —

Celui qui n'est pas chrétien au contraire, celui qui n'est
pas compétent en chrétienté, en matière de chrétienté, celui
qui est étranger c'est celui au contraire qui n'est point pécheur,
littéralement c'est celui qui ne commet aucun péché. Qui ne
peut commettre aucun péché. Littéralement celui qui est
pécheur, celui qui commet un péché est déjà chrétien, est en
cela même chrétien. On pourrait presque dire est un bon
chrétien. —

Le pécheur, ensemble avec le saint, entre dans le système,
est du système de chrétienté.

Celui qui n'entre pas dans le système, celui qui ne donne
pas la main, c'est celui-là qui n'est pas chrétien, c'est celui-là
qui n'a aucune compétence en matière de chrétienté. C'est
celui-là qui est un étranger. Le pécheur tend la main au saint,
donne la main au saint, puisque le saint donne la main au
pécheur. Et tous ensemble, l'un par l'autre, l'un tirant l'autre,
ils remontent jusqu'à Jésus, ils font une chaîne qui remonte
jusqu'à Jésus, une chaîne aux doigts indéliables. Celui qui

confused the two questions. This misinterpretation would go to prove better and more instantaneously than any other that one does not understand, that one does not catch on, that one does not know what is being talked about, that one is totally incompetent, that one is foreign to the question. No one, on the other hand, was less foreign, no one was as competent as Villon in matters of Christianity. Again, no one is more competent than a sinner in matters of Christianity. No one, unless it be a saint. And, in principle, it is the selfsame man.—

The sinner and the saint are, one can say, two portions equally integral, two equally integral parts of the Christian mechanism. One and the other, together, form two parts equally indispensable one to the other, two mutually complementary parts.—

He, on the other hand, who is not competent in Christianity, in matters of Christianity, is not a Christian. He, on the other hand, who is a stranger to this is not a sinner. Literally it is he who commits no sin, who can commit no sin. Literally he who is a sinner, he who commits sins is already a Christian, is in that respect himself a Christian. One could almost say a good Christian.—

The sinner, together with the saint, enters into the system, is of the system of Christianity.

He who does not enter into the system, he who does not hold out a hand, he it is who is not a Christian. It is he who has no competence whatever in matters of Christianity. It is he who is a stranger. The sinner holds out a hand to the saint, gives a hand to the saint, since the saint gives a hand to the sinner. And all together, one by means of the other, one pulling up the other, they ascend to Jesus, they form a chain which ascends to Jesus, a chain of fingers which cannot

n'est pas chrétien, c'est celui qui ne donne pas la main. Peu importe ce qu'il fasse ensuite de cette main. Quand un homme peut accomplir la plus haute action du monde sans avoir été trempé de la grâce, cet homme est un stoïque, il n'est pas un chrétien. Quand un homme peut commettre la plus basse action du monde précisément sans commettre un péché, cet homme n'est pas un chrétien. Le chrétien ne se définit point par l'étiage, mais par la communion. On n'est point chrétien parce qu'on est à un certain niveau, moral, intellectuel, spirituel même. On est chrétien parce qu'on est d'une certaine race remontante, d'une certaine race mystique, d'une certaine race spirituelle et charnelle, temporelle et éternelle, d'un certain sang. Ce classement cardinal ne se fait point horizontalement mais verticalement.

Quand un homme ne pèche pas, ne peut pas pécher, quand un homme peut commettre un crime sans que ce crime soit un péché, il n'est pas chrétien, c'est alors qu'il n'est pas chrétien, cet homme n'entre pas dans le système de chrétienté.

C'est une cité. Un mauvais citoyen est de la cité. Un bon étranger n'en est pas.

Ce qu'il y a de plus contrarié au salut même, ce n'est pas le péché, c'est l'habitude.

Il faut une religion pour le peuple — ce qui est bien, en un sens, l'injure la plus profonde que l'on ait jamais adressée à notre foi.

be unlinked. He who is not a Christian is he who does not hold out a hand. It matters little what next he does with this hand. When a man can accomplish the loftiest action in the world without being steeped in grace, this man is a Stoic, he is not a Christian. When a man can commit the lowest action in the world precisely without committing a sin, this man is not a Christian. A Christian is not defined by a low water mark, but by communion. One is not a Christian because of standing at a certain moral, intellectual, even a spiritual level. One is a Christian because of belonging to a certain ascending race, a certain mystic race, a certain spiritual and carnal race, temporal and eternal, belonging to a certain kindred. This cardinal classification cannot be made horizontally, but vertically.

When a man does not sin, cannot sin, when a man can commit a crime without this crime being a sin, he is not a Christian. It is then that he is not a Christian. This man does not enter the system of Christianity.

It is a city. A bad citizen belongs to the city. A good stranger does not.

WHAT IS MOST CONTRARY to salvation is not sin but habit.

A RELIGION IS NECESSARY for the people—this is, in a certain sense, the deepest insult that has ever been offered to our faith.

DE LA SAINTETE

IL EST EVIDENT qu'il y a infiniment plus de saints obscurs que de saints publics. Nous savons de toutes parts qu'il y a eu d'innombrables saints secrets. — Nous savons de certain qu'un très grand nombre de saints n'ont pas eu de vie publique et que la Gloire du ciel est la première qu'ils aient touchée.

Innombrable est la légion des chrétiens et des saints et il faut dire des martyrs qui ont été éprouvés dans le privé, qui n'ont pas été éprouvés publiquement. Or nous savons comme une des propositions les plus fermes de notre foi que Dieu ne fait aucune différence entre les uns et les autres et qu'ils reçoivent les mêmes couronnes. C'est une des propositions les plus fermes de notre foi que les mesures éternelles ne sont aucunement les mesures temporelles; que ni les récompenses ni les peines ni les couronnements d'aucune sorte ne se mesurent à nos inscriptions temporelles; qu'un pauvre homme dans son lit, que le dernier des malades peut au regard de Dieu, (et la chrétienté tout entière l'ignorant jusqu'au Jugement), mériter secrètement plus que le plus glorieux des saints. — Ce n'est pas seulement la grandeur, c'est le propre de notre foi que la sainteté, que la grâce opère avec un minimum de matière

OF SANCTITY

IT IS OBVIOUS THAT there are infinitely more obscure saints than public saints. We know from all sides that there have been innumerable secret saints.—We know for certain that a very great number of saints have had no public life and that the Glory in heaven is the first which they attained.

Innumerable is the legion of Christians and saints and, it must be said, of martyrs, who have been tried privately, who have not been tried publicly. Now we recognize as one of the stoutest prepositions of our faith that God makes no difference between the ones and the others, and that they receive the same crowns. It is one of the stoutest prepositions of our faith that eternal standards are in no way temporal standards; that neither rewards nor penalties, nor crowns can in any way be measured by our temporal records; that a poor man in his bed, that the last among the sick, in the eyes of God (and the whole of Christendom may be in ignorance of it until Judgement Day), can secretly deserve more than the most glorious among the saints. It is not greatness alone, it is the essence of our faith that sanctity, that grace operates with a minimum of temporal matter—and even that it is

temporelle et même qu'elle n'est jamais si à l'aise et si elle-même que dans le minimum de matière temporelle. Une liaison si parfaite unit le dernier des membres au Chef Couronné que le dernier des malades, dans son lit, est admis à imiter la souffrance même de Jésus en croix. Le dernier des malades, dans son lit, imite littéralement, imite effectivement, imite efficacement la Passion même de Jésus, le martyre de Jésus et des autres saints et martyrs. —

Le dernier des malades peut, par une sorte d'affectation à Dieu, de consécration à Dieu, tourner sa maladie en martyre, faire de sa maladie la matière même d'un martyre. —

Il ne fait aucun doute, et les saints le savaient bien, qu'il y a une sorte d'accointance propre entre la sainteté et la petite vie, une convenance particulière, propre, un goût de la grâce pour le secret, pour la vertu secrète, une accointance de Dieu pour l'humilité, — une accointance propre de Jésus pour les pauvres et les misérables et les humbles et les obscurs et les non publics. Tous les Evangiles regorgent d'une tendresse propre de Jésus pour les non publics. Tout le monde sent bien que les pauvres et les obscurs sont les favoris dans le royaume de Dieu. Ça en serait presque injuste s'il n'était loisible à tout le monde d'être pauvre.

never so much at ease and so much itself as in a minimum of temporal matter. Such a perfect bond links the last of the members to the crowned Chief that the last among the sick, in his bed, is admitted to imitate the suffering itself of Jesus on the Cross. The last among the sick in his bed literally imitates, effectively imitates, efficiently imitates the Passion itself of Jesus, the martyrdom of Jesus, and of the other saints and martyrs.—

The last among the sick can, by a kind of aspiration to God, a consecration to God, turn his sickness into martyrdom, make of the sickness itself the selfsame substance of martyrdom.—

There is no doubt, and the saints knew it well, that there is a sort of intimacy proper between sanctity and a humble life, a particular fitness proper to it, a taste of grace for the secret, for secret virtue, a close association of God with humility, a close association of Jesus with the poor and the wretched and the humble and the obscure and the non-public. All the Gospels overflow with the particular tenderness of Jesus for the non-public. Everyone is well aware that the poor are favorites in the kingdom of God. It would be almost unfair if it were not lawful for everyone to be poor.

POESIE

POETRY

LA DÉTRESSE DE LA FRANCE

JEANNE D'ARC PARLE :

Notre père, notre père qui êtes aux cieux, de combien il
s'en faut que votre volonté soit faite; de combien il s'en faut
que nous ayons notre pain de chaque jour.

De combien il s'en faut que nous pardonnions nos offenses;
et que nous ne succombions pas à la tentation; et que nous
soyons délivrés du mal. Ainsi soit-il.

O mon Dieu si on voyait seulement le commencement de
votre règne. Si on voyait seulement se lever le soleil de votre
règne. Mais rien, jamais rien. Vous nous avez envoyé votre
Fils, que vous aimiez tant, votre fils est venu, qui a tant
souffert, et il est mort, et rien, jamais rien. Si on voyait
poindre seulement le jour de votre règne. Et vous avez envoyé
vos saints, vous les avez appelés chacun par leur nom, vos
autres fils les saints, et vos filles les saintes, et vos saints sont
venus, et vos saintes sont venues, et rien, jamais rien. Des
années ont passé, tant d'années que je n'en sais pas le nombre;
des siècles d'années ont passé; quatorze siècles de chrétienté,
hélas, depuis la naissance, et la mort, et la prédication. Et
rien, rien, jamais rien. Et ce qui règne sur la face de la terre,

THE PLIGHT OF FRANCE

JOAN OF ARC SPEAKS:

Our father, our father who art in heaven, how far is your will from being done; how far are we from being given our daily bread.

How far are we from forgiving those who trespass against us; and not succumbing to temptation; and being delivered from evil. Amen.

O God if we could see only the beginning of your kingdom. If we could only see the sun of your kingdom rise. But there is nothing, there is never anything. You have sent us your son whom you loved so dearly, your son came, who suffered so much, and died. And now, nothing. There is never anything. If only we could see the daybreak of your kingdom. And you have sent us your saints, you have called each one of them by his name, your other sons the saints and your daughters the saints, and your saints have come, men and women, and now, nothing, there is never anything. Years have gone by, so many years that I cannot count them; centuries of years have gone by; fourteen centuries of christianity, alas, since the nativity, and the death, and the preaching.

rien, rien, ce n'est rien que la perdition. Quatorze siècles
(furent-ils de chrétienté), quatorze siècles depuis le rachat de
nos âmes. Et rien, jamais rien, le règne de la terre n'est rien
que le règne de la perdition, le royaume de la terre n'est rien
que le royaume de la perdition. Vous nous avez envoyé votre
fils et les autres saints. Et rien ne coule sur la face de la terre,
qu'un flot d'ingratitude et de perdition. Mon Dieu, mon Dieu,
faudra-t-il que votre Fils soit mort en vain. Il serait venu; et
cela ne servirait de rien. C'est pire que jamais. Seulement si
on voyait seulement se lever le soleil de votre justice. Mais on
dirait, mon Dieu, mon Dieu, pardonnez-moi, on dirait que
votre règne s'en va. Jamais on n'a tant blasphémé votre nom.
Jamais on n'a tant méprisé votre volonté. Jamais on n'a tant
désobéi. Jamais notre pain ne nous a tant manqué; et s'il ne
manquait qu'à nous, mon Dieu, s'il ne manquait qu'à nous;
et s'il n'y avait que le pain du corps qui nous manquait, le
pain de maïs, le pain de seigle et de blé; mais un autre pain
nous manque; le pain de la nourriture de nos âmes; et nous
sommes affamés d'une autre faim; de la seule faim qui laisse
dans le ventre un creux impérissable. Un autre pain nous
manque. Et au lieu que ce soit le règne de votre charité, le
seul règne qui règne sur la face de la terre, de votre terre, de
la terre votre création, au lieu que ce soit le règne du royaume
de votre charité, le seul règne qui règne, c'est le règne du
royaume impérissable du péché. Encore si l'on voyait le commencement de vos saints, si l'on voyait poindre le commencement du règne de vos saints. Mais qu'est-ce qu'on a fait, mon
Dieu, qu'est-ce qu'on a fait de votre créature, qu'est-ce qu'on
a fait de votre création ? Jamais il n'a été fait tant d'offenses;
et jamais tant d'offenses ne sont mortes impardonnées. Jamais
le chrétien n'a fait tant d'offense au chrétien, et jamais à vous,

And now, nothing, nothing, ever. And what reigns on the face of the earth is nothing, nothing, is nothing but perdition. Fourteen centuries (were they of christianity), fourteen centuries since the redemption of our souls. And nothing, nothing, ever, the reign of the earth is nothing but the reign of perdition, the kingdom of the earth is nothing but the kingdom of perdition. You have sent us your son and the other saints. And nothing flows down upon the face of the earth but a stream of ingratitude and perdition. God, God, will it have to be that your son died in vain? That he should have come and come in vain? It is worse than ever. Only, if we could only see the sun of your justice rise. But it looks as if, God, God, forgive me, it looks as if your reign were passing away. Never has your name been so blasphemed. Never has your will been so despised. Never has there been such disobedience. Never have we so much lacked our bread; and if we were the only ones to lack it, God, if we were the only ones; and if it were only the bread of the body which we lacked, the corn bread, the rye and wheat bread; but there is another bread which we lack, the bread for the nourishment of our souls; and we are hungry with another hunger, with the only hunger which leaves an everlasting hollow in our stomachs. There is another bread which we lack. And instead of the reign of your charity, the only reign reigning on the face of the earth, the earth of your creation, instead of the reign of the kingdom of your charity, we have the reign of the imperishable kingdom of sin. If we could at least see the beginning of your saints, if we could see the dawn of the beginning of this reign of your saints. But, God, what have they done, what have they done with your creature, what have they done with your creation? Never have so many

mon Dieu, jamais l'homme ne vous a fait tant d'offense. Et jamais tant d'offense n'est morte impardonnée. Sera-t-il dit que vous nous aurez envoyé en vain votre fils, et que votre fils aura souffert en vain, et qu'il sera mort. Et faudra-t-il que ce soit en vain qu'il se sacrifie et que nous le sacrifions tous les jours. Sera-ce en vain qu'une croix a été dressée un jour et que nous autres nous la redressons tous les jours. Qu'est-ce qu'on a fait du peuple chrétien, mon Dieu, de votre peuple. Et ce ne sont plus seulement les tentations qui nous assiègent, mais ce sont les tentations qui triomphent; et ce sont les tentations qui règnent; et c'est le règne de la tentation; et le règne des royaumes de la terre est tombé tout entier au règne du royaume de la tentation; et les mauvais succombent à la tentation du mal, de faire du mal; de faire du mal aux autres; et pardonnez-moi, mon Dieu, de vous faire du mal à vous; mais les bons, ceux qui étaient bons, succombent à une tentation infiniment pire: à la tentation de croire qu'ils sont abandonnés de vous. Au nom du Père, et du Fils, et du Saint-Esprit, mon Dieu délivrez-nous du mal, délivrez-nous du mal. S'il n'y a pas eu encore assez de saintes et assez de saints, envoyez-nous en d'autres, envoyez-nous en autant qu'il en faudra; envoyez-nous en tant que l'ennemi se lasse. Nous les suivrons, mon Dieu. Nous ferons tout ce que vous voudrez. Nous ferons tout ce qu'ils voudront. Nous ferons tout ce qu'ils nous diront de votre part. Nous sommes vos fidèles, envoyez-nous vos saints; nous sommes vos brebis, envoyez-nous vos bergers; nous sommes le troupeau, envoyez-nous les pasteurs. Nous sommes des bons chrétiens, vous savez que nous sommes des bons chrétiens. Alors comment que ça se fait que tant de bons chrétiens ne fassent pas une bonne chrétienté. Il faut qu'il y ait quelque chose qui ne marche pas. Si vous nous envoyiez,

trespassed and never have so many trespasses died unforgiven. Never has Christian trespassed so much against
Christian, and against you, God, never has man trespassed
so much against you. And never has so much trespassing died
unforgiven. Will it be said that you have sent us your son
in vain, and that your son has suffered in vain, and that he
has died. And will it have to be in vain that he sacrifices himself and that we sacrifice him every day. Will it be in vain
that a cross was set up one day and that we set it up again
every day. What have they done with the Christian people,
God, what have they done with your people. And not only
do temptations besiege us, but temptations triumph, and temptations reign, and it is the reign of temptation, and the reign
of the kingdoms of the earth has altogether fallen into the
reign of the kingdom of temptation, and the evil succumb
to the temptation of evil, the temptation to do evil, to do evil
to others, and, God, forgive me, to do evil to you; but the
good, who were good, succumb to a temptation infinitely
worse: the temptation to believe that they have been for-
saken by you. In the name of the Father, and of the Son, and
of the Holy Ghost, Lord, deliver us from evil, deliver us
from evil. If there have not yet been enough saints, men and
women, send us some more, send us as many as will be
needed, send us so many that the enemy will get tired. We
will follow them, God. We will do everything you wish. We
will do everything they wish. We will do everything they tell
us in your name. We are your faithful, send us your saints;
we are your sheep, send us your shepherds; we are the flock,
send us the pastors. We are good Christians, you know that
we are good Christians. So how is it that so many good
Christians don't make up a good Christendom. There must

si seulement vous vouliez nous envoyer l'une de vos saintes.
Il y en a bien encore. On dit qu'il y en a. On en voit. On en
sait. On en connaît. Mais on ne sait pas comment que ça se
fait. Il y a des saintes, il y a de la sainteté, et ça ne marche pas
tout de même. Il y a quelque chose qui ne marche pas. Il y a
des saintes, il y a de la sainteté et jamais le règne du royaume
de la perdition n'avait autant dominé sur la face de la terre.
Il faudrait peut-être autre chose, mon Dieu, vous savez tout.
Vous savez ce qui nous manque. Il nous faudrait peut-être
quelque chose de nouveau, quelque chose qu'on n'aurait encore jamais vu. Quelque chose qu'on n'aurait encore jamais
fait. Mais qui oserait dire, mon Dieu, qu'il puisse encore y
avoir du nouveau après quatorze siècles de chrétienté, après
tant de saintes et tant de saints, après tous vos martyrs, après
la passion et la mort de votre fils.

Enfin ce qu'il nous faudrait, mon Dieu, il faudrait nous
envoyer une sainte... qui réussisse.

be something wrong. If you could send us, if only you would send us one of your holy women. There are still some. People say that there are. Some have been seen. Some are heard of. Some are known. But we don't know how it is managed. There are saints among women, there is holiness, and yet it doesn't seem to work. There is something which doesn't work. There are saints among women, there is holiness and never did the reign of the kingdom of perdition so entirely dominate the face of the earth. Perhaps something else is needed, God, you know everything. You know what we lack. Perhaps we need something new, something no one has ever seen. Something no one has ever done. But who would dare say, God, that there could be anything new after fourteen centuries of Christianity, after so many saints, men and women, after all your martyrs, after the passion and death of your son.

What we need, God, what we finally need is a woman who would also be a saint . . . and who would succeed.

GUERRE

JEANNE D'ARC PARLE :

Savez-vous que nous, qui voyons tout cela se passer sous nos yeux sans rien faire à présent que des charités vaines, — puisque nous ne voulons pas tuer la guerre, nous sommes les complices de tout cela ? Nous qui laissons faire les soldats, savez-vous que, nous aussi, nous sommes les tourmenteuses des corps et les damneuses des âmes. Nous aussi, nous mêmes, nous souffletons Jésus en croix. Nous aussi, nous mêmes nous profanons le corps impérissable de Jésus.

Complice, complice, c'est comme auteur. Nous en sommes les complices, nous en sommes les auteurs. Complice, complice, c'est autant dire auteur.

Celui qui laisse faire est comme celui qui fait faire. C'est tout un. Ça va ensemble. Et celui qui laisse faire et celui qui fait faire ensemble c'est comme celui qui fait, c'est autant que celui qui fait. C'est pire que celui qui fait. Car celui qui fait, il a au moins le courage de faire. Celui qui commet un crime, il a au moins le courage de le commettre. Et quand on le laisse faire, il y a le même crime, c'est le même crime; et il y a la lâcheté par dessus. Il y a la lâcheté en plus.

Il y a partout une lâcheté infinie.

W A R

J O A N O F A R C S P E A K S :

Do you know that we, who see all this going on under our eyes and are content at present with empty charities, since we do not want to kill war, do you know that we are accomplices in all this? We who let the soldiers do as they wish, do you know that we too torment bodies and damn souls? We too, even we, strike crucified Jesus on the cheek. We too, even we, profane the imperishable body of Jesus.

An accomplice, an accomplice, it's like an author. We are accomplices in this, we are the authors of this. Accomplice, accomplice, it is just as if you said author.

He who allows things to be done is like him who orders them to be done. It is all one. It goes together. And he who allows things to be done, just like him who orders them to be done, it is altogether like him who does them. Because he who does shows courage, at least, in doing. He who commits a crime has at least the courage to commit it. And when you allow the crime to be committed, you have the same crime, and cowardice to boot. Cowardice on top of it all.

There is everywhere infinite cowardice.

LIBERTE

DIEU PARLE :

Quand on aime un être, on l'aime comme il est.
Il n'y a que moi qui est parfait.
C'est même pour cela peut-être
Que je sais ce que c'est que la perfection
Et que je demande moins de perfection à ces pauvres gens.
Je sais, moi, combien c'est difficile.
Et combien de fois quand ils peinent tant dans leurs épreuves
J'ai envie, je suis tenté de leur mettre la main sous le ventre
Pour les soutenir dans ma large main
Comme un père qui apprend à nager à son fils
Dans le courant de la rivière
Et qui est partagé entre deux sentiments.
Car d'une part s'il le soutient toujours et s'il le soutient trop
L'enfant s'y fiera et il n'apprendra jamais à nager.
Mais aussi s'il ne le soutient pas juste au bon moment
Cet enfant boira un mauvais coup.

FREEDOM

GOD SPEAKS:

When you love someone, you love him as he is.
I alone am perfect.
It is probably for that reason
That I know what perfection is
And that I demand less perfection of those poor people.
I know how difficult it is.
And how often, when they are struggling in their trials,
How often do I wish and am I tempted to put my hand under
    their stomachs
In order to hold them up with my big hand
Just like a father teaching his son how to swim
In the current of the river
And who is divided between two ways of thinking.
For on the one hand, if he holds him up all the time and if
    he holds him up too much,
The child will depend on this and will never learn how to
    swim.
But if he doesn't hold him up just at the right moment
That child is bound to swallow more water than is healthy
    for him.

Ainsi moi quand je leur apprends à nager dans leurs épreuves
Moi aussi je suis partagé entre ces deux sentiments.
Car si je les soutiens toujours et je les soutiens trop
Ils ne sauront jamais nager eux-mêmes.
Mais si je ne les soutiens pas juste au bon moment
Ces pauvres enfants boiraient peut-être un mauvais coup.
Telle est la difficulté, elle est grande.
Et telle la duplicité même, la double face du problème.
D'une part il faut qu'ils fassent leur salut eux-mêmes. C'est
    la règle.
Et elle est formelle. Autrement ce ne serait pas intéressant.
    Ils ne seraient pas des hommes.
Or je veux qu'ils soient virils, qu'ils soient des hommes et
    qu'ils gagnent eux-mêmes
Leurs éperons de chevaliers.
D'autre part il ne faut pas qu'ils boivent un mauvais coup
Ayant fait un plongeon dans l'ingratitude du péché.
Tel est le mystère de la liberté de l'homme, dit Dieu,
Et de mon gouvernement envers lui et envers sa liberté.
Si je le soutiens trop, il n'est plus libre
Et si je ne le soutiens pas assez, j'expose son salut :
Deux biens en un sens presque également précieux.
Car ce salut a un prix infini.

In the same way, when I teach them how to swim amid their
 trials

I too am divided by two ways of thinking.

Because if I am always holding them up, if I hold them up
 too often,

They will never learn how to swim by themselves.

But if I don't hold them up just at the right moment,

Perhaps those poor children will swallow more water than is
 healthy for them.

Such is the difficulty, and it is a great one.

And such is the doubleness itself, the two faces of the problem.

On the one hand, they must work out their salvation for themselves. That is the rule.

It allows of no exception. Otherwise it would not be interest-
 ing. They would not be men.

Now I want them to be manly, to be men, and to win by
 themselves

Their spurs of knighthood.

On the other hand, they must not swallow more water than is
 healthy for them,

Having made a dive into the ingratitude of sin.

Such is the mystery of man's freedom, says God,

And the mystery of my government towards him and towards
 his freedom.

If I hold him up too much, he is no longer free

And if I don't hold him up sufficiently, I am endangering his
 salvation.

Two goods in a sense almost equally precious.

For salvation is of infinite price.

Mais qu'est-ce qu'un salut qui ne serait pas libre

Comment serait-il qualifié.

Nous voulons que ce salut soit acquis par lui-même.

Par lui-même l'homme. Soit procuré par lui-même.

Vienne en un sens de lui-même. Tel est le secret,

Tel est le mystère de la liberté de l'homme.

Tel est le prix que nous mettons à la liberté de l'homme.

Parce que moi-même je suis libre, dit Dieu, et que j'ai créé
l'homme à mon image et à ma ressemblance.

Tel est le mystère, tel est le secret, tel est le prix

De toute liberté.

Cette liberté de cette créature est le plus beau reflet qu'il y ait
dans le monde

De la Liberté du Créateur. C'est pour cela que nous y
attachons,

Que nous y mettons un prix propre.

Un salut qui ne serait pas libre, qui ne serait pas, qui ne
viendrait pas d'un homme libre ne nous dirait plus rien.
Qu'est-ce que ce serait.

Qu'est-ce que ça voudrait dire.

Quel intérêt un tel salut présenterait-il.

Une béatitude d'esclaves, un salut d'esclaves, une béatitude
serve, en quoi voulez-vous que ça m'intéresse. Aime-t-on
à être aimé par des esclaves.

S'il ne s'agit que de faire la preuve de ma puissance, ma
puissance n'a pas besoin de ces esclaves, ma puissance est
assez connue, on sait assez que je suis le Tout-Puissant.

Ma puissance éclate assez dans toute matière et dans tout
événement.

Ma puissance éclate assez dans les sables de la mer et dans
les étoiles du ciel.

But what kind of salvation would a salvation be that was not
  free?
What would you call it?
We want that salvation to be acquired by himself,
Himself, man. To be procured by himself.
To come, in a sense, from himself. Such is the secret,
Such is the mystery of man's freedom.
Such is the price we set on man's freedom.
Because I myself am free, says God, and I have created man
  in my own image and likeness.
Such is the mystery, such the secret, such the price
Of all freedom.
That freedom of that creature is the most beautiful reflection
  in this world
Of the Creator's freedom. That is why we are so attached to it,
And set a proper price on it.
A salvation that was not free, that was not, that did not come
  from a free man could in no wise be attractive to us. What
  would it amount to?
What would it mean?
What interest would such a salvation have to offer?
A beatitude of slaves, a salvation of slaves, a slavish beati-
  tude, how do you expect me to be interested in that kind of
  thing? Does one care to be loved by slaves?
If it were only a matter of proving my might, my might has
  no need of those slaves, my might is well enough known,
  it is sufficiently known that I am the Almighty.
My might is manifest enough in all matter and in all events.
My might is manifest enough in the sands of the sea and in
  the stars of heaven.

Elle n'est point contestée, elle est connue, elle éclate assez
   dans la création inanimée.
Elle éclate assez dans le gouvernement,
Dans l'événement même de l'homme.
Mais dans ma création animée, dit Dieu, j'ai voulu mieux, j'ai
   voulu plus.
Infiniment mieux. Infiniment plus. Car j'ai voulu cette liberté.
J'ai créé cette liberté même. Il y a plusieurs degrés de mon
   trône.
Quand une fois on a connu d'être aimé librement, les soumis-
   sions n'ont plus aucun goût. —
Tous les prosternements du monde
Ne valent pas le bel agenouillement droit d'un homme libre.
   Toutes les soumissions, tous les accablements du monde
Ne valent pas le point d'élancement,
Le bel élancement droit d'une seule invocation
D'un libre amour.

It is not questioned, it is known, it is manifest enough in
    inanimate creation.
It is manifest enough in the government,
In the very event that is man.
But in my creation which is endued with life, says God, I
    wanted something better, I wanted something more.
Infinitely better. Infinitely more. For I wanted that freedom.
I created that very freedom. There are several degrees to my
    throne.
When you once have known what it is to be loved freely,
    submission no longer has any taste.
All the prostrations in the world
Are not worth the beautiful upright attitude of a free man
    as he kneels. All the submission, all the dejection in the
    world
Are not equal in value to the soaring up point,
The beautiful straight soaring up of one single invocation
From a love that is free.

SOMMEIL

DIEU PARLE :

Je n'aime pas celui qui ne dort pas, dit Dieu.
Le sommeil est l'ami de l'homme.
Le sommeil est l'ami de Dieu.
Le sommeil est peut-être ma plus belle création.
Et moi-même je me suis reposé le septième jour.
Celui qui a le cœur pur, dort. Et celui qui dort a le cœur pur.
C'est le grand secret d'être infatigable comme un enfant.
D'avoir comme un enfant cette force dans les jarrets.
Ces jarrets neufs, ces âmes neuves
Et de recommencer tous les matins, toujours neuf,
Comme la jeune, comme la neuve
Espérance. Or on me dit qu'il y a des hommes
Qui travaillent bien et qui dorment mal.
Qui ne dorment pas. Quel manque de confiance en moi.
C'est presque plus grave que s'ils travaillaient mal mais dor-
   maient bien.
Que s'ils ne travaillaient pas mais dormaient, car la paresse
N'est pas un plus grand péché que l'inquiétude
Et même c'est un moins grand péché que l'inquiétude
Et que le désespoir et le manque de confiance en moi.

SLEEP

GOD SPEAKS:

I don't like the man who doesn't sleep, says God.
Sleep is the friend of man.
Sleep is the friend of God.
Sleep is perhaps the most beautiful thing I have created.
And I myself rested on the seventh day.
He whose heart is pure, sleeps. And he who sleeps has a pure
    heart.
That is the great secret of being as indefatigable as a child.
Of having that strength in the legs that a child has.
Those new legs, those new souls,
And to begin afresh every morning, ever new,
Like young hope, new hope.
But they tell me that there are men
Who work well and sleep badly.
Who don't sleep. What a lack of confidence in me.
It is almost more serious than if they worked badly and slept
    well.
Than if they did not work but slept, because laziness
Is not a greater sin than unrest,
It is not even so great a sin as unrest
And despair and lack of confidence in me.

Je ne parle pas, dit Dieu, de ces hommes
Qui ne travaillent pas et qui ne dorment pas.
Ceux-là sont des pécheurs, c'est entendu. C'est bien fait pour
eux.
Des grands pécheurs. Ils n'ont qu'à travailler.
Je parle de ceux qui travaillent et qui ne dorment pas.
Je les plains. Je parle de ceux qui travaillent, et qui ainsi
En ceci suivent mon commandement, les pauvres enfants.
Et qui d'autre part n'ont pas le courage, n'ont pas la confiance,
ne dorment pas.
Je les plains. Je leur en veux. Un peu. Ils ne me font pas
confiance.
Comme l'enfant se couche innocent dans les bras de sa mère
ainsi ils ne se couchent point
Innocents dans les bras de ma Providence.
Ils ont le courage de travailler. Ils n'ont pas le courage de ne
rien faire.
Ils ont la vertu de travailler. Ils n'ont pas la vertu de ne rien
faire.
De se détendre. De se reposer. De dormir.
Les malheureux ils ne savent pas ce qui est bon.
Ils gouvernent très bien leurs affaires pendant le jour.
Mais ils ne veulent pas m'en confier le gouvernement pendant
la nuit.
Comme si je n'étais pas capable d'en assurer le gouvernement
pendant une nuit.
Celui qui ne dort pas est infidèle à l'Espérance.
Et c'est la plus grande infidélité.
Parce que c'est l'infidélité à la plus grande Foi.
Pauvres enfants ils administrent dans la journée leurs affaires
avec sagesse.

I am not talking, says God, about those men
Who don't work and don't sleep.
Those men are sinners, to be sure. They have what they
    deserve.
Great sinners. It's their fault for not working.
I am talking about those who work and don't sleep.
I pity them. I am talking about those who work and who, in
    this,
Obey my commandment, poor children.
And who on the other hand lack courage, lack confidence,
    and don't sleep.
I pity them. I have it against them. A little. They won't trust
    me.
Like the child who innocently lies in his mother's arms,
    thus do they not lie
Innocently in the arms of my Providence.
They have the courage to work. They lack the courage to be
    idle.
They have enough virtue to work. They haven't enough virtue
    to be idle.
To stretch out. To rest. To sleep.
Poor people, they don't know what is good.
They look after their business very well during the day.
But they haven't enough confidence in me to let me look after
    it during the night.
As if I wasn't capable of looking after it during one night.
He who doesn't sleep is unfaithful to Hope.
And it is the greatest infidelity.
Because it is infidelity to the greatest Faith.
Poor children, they conduct their business with wisdom dur-
    ing the day.

Mais le soir venu ils ne se résolvent point,

Ils ne se résignent point à en confier le gouvernement à ma
sagesse ——

Et l'administration et tout le gouvernement.

Comme si je n'étais pas capable, peut-être, de m'en occuper
un peu.

D'y veiller.

De gouverner et d'administrer et tout le tremblement.

J'en administre bien d'autres, pauvres gens, je gouverne la
création, c'est peut-être plus difficile.

Vous pourriez peut-être sans grand(s) dommage(s) me
laisser vos affaires en mains, hommes sages.

Je suis peut-être aussi sage que vous.

Vous pourriez peut-être me les remettre l'espace d'une nuit.

L'espace que vous dormiez

Enfin

Et le lendemain matin vous les retrouveriez peut-être pas trop
abîmées.

Le lendemain matin elles ne seraient peut-être pas plus mal.

Je suis peut-être encore capable de les conduire un peu. Je
parle de ceux qui travaillent

Et qui ainsi en ceci suivent mon commandement.

Et qui ne dorment pas, et qui ainsi en ceci

Refusent tout ce qu'il y a de bon dans ma création,

Le sommeil, tout ce que j'ai créé de bon,

Et aussi refusent tout de même ici mon commandement même.

Pauvres enfants quelle ingratitude envers moi

Que de refuser un aussi bon,

Un aussi beau commandement.

Pauvres enfants ils suivent la sagesse humaine.

But when evening comes, they can't make up their minds,
They can't be resigned to trust my wisdom for the space of
   one night
With the conduct and the governing of their business.
As if I wasn't capable, if you please, of looking after it a
   little.
Of watching over it.
Of governing and conducting, and all that kind of stuff.
I have a great deal more business to look after, poor people,
   I govern creation, maybe that is more difficult.
You might perhaps, and no harm done, leave your business
   in my hands, O wise men.
Maybe I am just as wise as you are.
You might perhaps leave it to me for the space of a night.
While you are asleep
At last
And the next morning you might find it not too badly dam-
   aged perhaps.
The next morning it might not be any the worse perhaps.
I may yet be capable of attending to it a little. I am talking
   of those who work
And who in this obey my commandment.
And don't sleep, and who in this
Refuse all that is good in my creation,
Sleep, all the good I have created,
And also refuse my commandment just the same.
Poor children, what ingratitude towards me
To refuse such a good
Such a beautiful commandment.
Poor children, they follow human wisdom.

La sagesse humaine dit Ne remettez pas au lendemain
Ce que vous pouvez faire le jour même.
Et moi je vous dis Celui qui sait remettre au lendemain
Est celui qui est le plus agréable à Dieu.
Celui qui dort comme un enfant
Est aussi celui qui dort comme ma chère Espérance.
Et moi je vous dis Remettez à demain
Ces soucis et ces peines qui aujourd'hui vous rongent
Et aujourd'hui pourraient vous dévorer.
Remettez à demain ces sanglots qui vous étouffent
Quand vous voyez le malheur d'aujourd'hui.
Ces sanglots qui vous montent et qui vous étranglent.
Remettez à demain ces larmes qui vous emplissent les yeux
et la tête.
Qui vous inondent. Qui vous tombent. Ces larmes qui vous
coulent.
Parce que d'ici demain, moi, Dieu, j'aurai peut-être passé.
La sagesse humaine dit: Malheureux qui remet à demain.
Et moi je dis Heureux, heureux qui remet à demain.
Heureux qui remet. C'est-à-dire Heureux qui espère. Et qui
dort.

Human wisdom says Don't put off until tomorrow
What can be done the very same day.
But I tell you that he who knows how to put off until to-
morrow
Is the most agreeable to God.
He who sleeps like a child
Is also he who sleeps like my darling Hope.
And I tell you Put off until tomorrow
Those worries and those troubles which are gnawing at you
today
And might very well devour you today.
Put off until tomorrow those sobs that choke you
When you see today's unhappiness.
Those sobs which rise up and strangle you.
Put off until tomorrow those tears which fill your eyes and
your head,
Flooding you, rolling down your cheeks, those tears which
stream down your cheeks.
Because between now and tomorrow, maybe I, God, will have
passed by your way.
Human wisdom says: Woe to the man who puts off what he
has to do until tomorrow.
And I say Blessed, blessed is the man who puts off what he
has to do until tomorrow.
Blessed is he who puts off. That is to say Blessed is he who
hopes. And who sleeps.

ABANDON

DIEU PARLE :

Je connais bien l'homme. C'est moi qui l'ai fait. C'est un drôle
   d'être.
Car en lui joue cette liberté qui est le mystère des mystères.
On peut encore lui demander beaucoup. Il n'est pas trop
   mauvais. Il ne faut pas dire qu'il est mauvais.
Quand on sait le prendre, on peut encore lui demander
   beaucoup.
Lui faire rendre beaucoup. Et Dieu sait si ma grâce
Sait le prendre, si avec ma grâce
Je sais le prendre. Si ma grâce est insidieuse, habile comme
   un voleur.
Et comme un homme qui chasse le renard.
Je sais le prendre. C'est mon métier. Et cette liberté même
   est ma création.
On peut lui demander beaucoup de cœur, beaucoup de charité,
   beaucoup de sacrifice.
Il a beaucoup de foi et beaucoup de charité.
Mais ce qu'on ne peut pas lui demander, sacredié, c'est un
   peu d'espérance.

A B A N D O N M E N T

G O D   S P E A K S :

I know man well. It is I who made him. A funny creature.
For in him that freedom is at work which is the mystery of
　　mysteries.
You can still ask a lot of him. He is not too bad. You can't
　　say that he is bad.
When you know how to handle him, you can still ask a lot
　　of him.
You can get a lot out of him. And God knows that my grace
Knows how to handle him, that with my grace
I know how to handle him, that my grace is insidious, as
　　clever as a thief
And like a man hunting a fox.
I know how to handle him. It's my business. And that free-
　　dom of his is my creation.
You can ask a lot of kindness of him, a lot of charity, a lot
　　of sacrifice.
He has much faith and much charity.
But what you can't ask of him, by gum, is a little hope.

Un peu de confiance, quoi, un peu de détente,

Un peu de remise, un peu d'abandonnement dans mes mains,

Un peu de désistement. Il se raidit tout le temps.

Or toi, ma fille la nuit, tu réussis, quelquefois, tu obtiens quelquefois cela

De l'homme rebelle.

Qu'il consente, ce monsieur, qu'il se rende un peu à moi.

Qu'il détende un peu ses pauvres membres las sur un lit de
repos.

Qu'il détende un peu sur un lit de repos son cœur endolori.

Que sa tête surtout ne marche plus. Elle ne marche que trop,
sa tête. Et il croit que c'est du travail, que sa tête marche
comme ça.

Et ses pensées, non, pour ce qu'il appelle ses pensées.

Que ses idées ne marchent plus et ne se battent plus dans sa
tête et ne grelottent plus comme des grains de calebasse,

Comme un grelot dans une courge vide.

Quand on voit ce que c'est, que ce qu'il appelle ses idées.

Pauvre être. Je n'aime pas, dit Dieu, l'homme qui ne dort pas.

Celui qui brûle, dans son lit, d'inquiétude et de fièvre.

Je suis partisan, dit Dieu, que tous les soirs on fasse son
examen de conscience.

C'est un bon exercice.

Mais enfin il ne faut pas s'en torturer au point d'en perdre
le sommeil.

A cette heure-là la journée est faite, et bien faite; il n'y a
plus à la refaire.

Il n'y a plus à y revenir.

A little confidence, don't you know, a little relaxation.

A little yielding, a little abandonment into my hands,

A little giving in. He is always so stiff.

Now you, my daughter night, you sometimes succeed, you sometimes obtain that very thing

Of rebellious man.

Let the gentleman consent, let him yield a little to me.

Let him stretch out his poor weary limbs on a bed of rest.

Let him ease his aching heart a little on a bed of rest.

Above all, let his head stop working. It works only too much, his head does. And he thinks it is work, when his head goes that way.

And his thoughts . . . Did you ever . . . What he calls his thoughts!

Let his thoughts stop moving about and struggling inside his head and rattling like calabash seeds,

Like a little bell in an empty gourd.

When you see what they are all about, those ideas of his, as he calls them!

Poor creature. I don't care for the man who doesn't sleep, says God.

The man who is all aglow in his bed, all aglow with unrest and fever.

I am all for making one's examination of conscience every night, says God.

It is a good exercise.

But after all, you mustn't torment yourself with it to the point of losing your sleep.

At that hour, the day is done, and well done. It doesn't have to be done over again.

It is all settled.

Ces péchés qui vous font tant de peine, mon garçon, eh bien
c'était bien simple,

Mon ami, il ne fallait pas les commettre,

A l'heure où tu pouvais encore ne pas les commettre.

A présent, c'est fait, va, dors, demain tu ne recommenceras
plus.

Mais celui qui le soir en se couchant fait des plans pour le
lendemain,

Celui-là je ne l'aime pas, dit Dieu.

Le sot, est-ce qu'il sait seulement comment demain sera fait?

Est-ce qu'il connaît seulement la couleur du temps?

Il ferait mieux de faire sa prière. Je n'ai jamais refusé le
pain du lendemain.

Celui qui est dans ma main comme le bâton dans la main du
voyageur,

Celui-là m'est agréable, dit Dieu.

Celui qui est posé dans mon bras comme un nourrisson qui rit,

Et qui ne s'occupe de rien,

Et qui voit le monde dans les yeux de sa mère, et de sa
nourrice,

Et qui ne le voit et ne le regarde que là,

Celui-là m'est agréable, dit Dieu.

Mais celui qui fait des combinaisons, celui qui en lui-même
pour demain dans sa tête

Travaille comme un mercenaire,

Travaille affreusement comme un esclave qui tourne une roue
éternelle,

(Et entre nous comme un imbécile),

Eh bien celui-là ne m'est pas agréable du tout, dit Dieu.

Celui qui s'abandonne, je l'aime. Celui qui ne s'abandonne
pas, je ne l'aime pas, c'est pourtant simple.

Those sins for which you are so sorry, my boy, well, it is
  plain enough,
My friend, you should not have committed them.
At the time when you were still free not to commit them.
Now it's over. So go to sleep, you won't do it again tomorrow.
But the man who, going to bed at night, makes plans for the
  next day,
That man I don't care for.
Jackass, how does he know what tomorrow will be like?
Does he even know what color the weather is going to take
  on?
He had much better say his prayers. I have never withheld
  tomorrow's bread.
The man who is in my hand like the staff in the traveller's
  hand,
That man is agreeable to me, says God.
The man who rests on my arm like the suckling child who
  laughs
And is not concerned with anything,
And sees the world in his mother's and his nurse's eyes,
And sees it nowhere else, and looks for it nowhere else,
That one is agreeable to me, says God.
But the one who concocts plans, the one who inside himself,
  in his own head,
Works for tomorrow like a hired laborer,
Works dreadfully like a slave making an everlasting wheel
  go round,
(And between you and me like a fool),
Well, that man is in no way agreeable to me, says God.
He who abandons himself, I love. He who does not abandon
  himself, I don't love. That's simple enough.

Celui qui s'abandonne ne s'abandonne pas et il est le seul qui
    ne s'abandonne pas.

Celui qui ne s'abandonne pas s'abandonne et il est le seul qui
    s'abandonne.

Or toi, ma fille la nuit, ma fille au grand manteau, ma fille au
    manteau d'argent,

Tu es la seule qui vaincs quelquefois ce rebelle et qui fais
    plier cette nuque dure.

C'est alors, ô Nuit, que tu viens.

Et ce que tu as fait une fois,

Tu le fais toutes les fois.

Ce que tu as fait un jour,

Tu le fais tous les jours.

Comme tu es tombée un soir,

Ainsi tu tombes tous les soirs.

Ce que tu as fait pour mon fils fait homme,

O grande Charitable tu le fais pour tous les hommes ses
    frères

Tu les ensevelis dans le silence et l'ombre

Et dans le salutaire oubli

De la mortelle inquiétude

Du jour.

He who abandons himself does not abandon himself, and he
  is the only one who does not abandon himself.

He who does not abandon himself, abandons himself, and is
  the only one who does abandon himself.

Now you, my daughter night, my daughter of the great cloak,
  my daughter of the silver cloak,

You are the only one who sometimes overcomes that rebel
  and can bend that stiff neck of his,

It is then, O night, that you appear.

And what you have done once,

You do every time.

What you have done one day,

You do every day.

As you came down one evening,

So you come down every evening.

What you did for my son who was made man,

O great and charitable one, you do for all men his brothers,

You bury them in silence and shadow

And in the salutary oblivion

Of the mortal unrest

Of day.

L'INNOCENCE ET L'EXPERIENCE

DIEU PARLE :

C'est l'innocence qui est pleine et c'est l'expérience qui est
   vide.
C'est l'innocence qui gagne et c'est l'expérience qui perd.

C'est l'innocence qui est jeune et c'est l'expérience qui est
   vieille.
C'est l'innocence qui croît et c'est l'expérience qui décroît.

C'est l'innocence qui naît et c'est l'expérience qui meurt.
C'est l'innocence qui sait et c'est l'expérience qui ne sait pas.

C'est l'enfant qui est plein et c'est l'homme qui est vide.
Vide comme une courge vide et comme un tonneau vide:

Voilà, dit Dieu, ce que j'en fais, de votre expérience.

Allez, mes enfants, allez à l'école.
Et vous, hommes, allez à l'école de la vie.
Allez apprendre
A désapprendre.

INNOCENCE AND EXPERIENCE

GOD SPEAKS:

It is innocence that is full and experience that is empty.
It is innocence that wins and experience that loses.

It is innocence that is young and experience that is old.
It is innocence that grows and experience that wanes.

It is innocence that is born and experience that dies.
It is innocence that knows and experience that does not know.

It is the child who is full and the man who is empty,
Empty as an empty gourd and as an empty barrel:

That is what I do with that experience of yours.

Now then, children, go to school.
And you men, go to the school of life.
Go and learn
How to unlearn.

Toute histoire s'est jouée deux fois, dit Dieu: une fois en
 juiverie.

Et une fois en chrétiennerie. L'enfant (Jésus) s'est joué deux
 fois.

Une fois en Benjamin et une fois dans l'enfant Jésus.

Et l'enfant perdu et la brebis perdue et la drachme perdue
 s'est jouée deux fois.

Et la première fois ce fut dans Joseph, *je suis Joseph votre
 frère.*

Il fallait que cela fût joué, dit Dieu. Et deux fois plutôt qu'une.

Car il y a dans l'enfant, car il y a dans l'enfance une grâce
 unique.

Une entièreté, une premièreté

Totale.

Une origine, un secret, une source, un point d'origine.

Un commencement pour ainsi dire absolu.

Les enfants sont des créatures neuves.

Eux aussi, eux surtout, eux premiers ils prennent le ciel de
 force.

Rapiunt, ils ravissent. Mais quelle douce violence.

Et quelle agréable force et quelle tendresse de force.

Comme un père endure volontiers

Comme il aime à endurer les violences de cette force,

Les embrassements de cette tendresse.

Pour moi, dit Dieu, je ne connais rien d'aussi beau dans tout
 le monde

Qu'un gamin d'enfant qui cause avec le bon Dieu

Dans le fond d'un jardin.

Et qui fait les demandes et les réponses (C'est plus sûr).

Un petit homme qui raconte ses peines au bon Dieu

Le plus sérieusement du monde.

All history was enacted twice, says God: once in Jewry,

And once in Christendom. The child (Jesus) was twice enacted,

Once in Benjamin and once in the child Jesus.

And the lost child and the lost sheep and the lost drachma,
all were twice enacted.

And the first time, it was in Joseph, *I am Joseph your brother.*

It had to be enacted, says God. Twice rather than once.

Because there is in the child, there is in childhood a unique
grace,

An entirety, a firstness

That is total,

An origin, a secret, a spring, a point of departure,

A beginning which might be called absolute.

Children are new creatures.

They too, they in particular, they first among all take heaven
by force.

Rapiunt, they ravish. But with what sweet violence!

And what agreeable force and what tenderness of force!

Just as a father willingly submits,

How he loves to submit to the violence of that strength!

To the embraces of that tenderness!

As for me, says God, I know nothing so beautiful in the whole
world

As a mere child having a talk with the good Lord

At the bottom of the garden;

Asking questions and giving the answers himself (it's safer
that way).

A little man telling the good Lord about his woes,

As seriously as anyone in the world,

Et qui se fait lui-même les consolations du bon Dieu.
Or je vous le dis, ces consolations qu'il se fait.
Elles viennent directement et proprement de moi. —

Rien n'est beau comme un enfant qui s'endort en faisant sa
   prière, dit Dieu.
Je vous le dis, rien n'est aussi beau dans le monde. —
Et pourtant j'en ai vu des beautés dans le monde
Et je m'y connais. Ma création regorge de beautés.
Ma création regorge de merveilles.
Il y en a tant qu'on ne sait pas où les mettre.
J'ai vu des millions et des millions d'astres rouler sous mes
   pieds comme les sables de la mer.
J'ai vu des journées ardentes comme des flammes,
Des jours d'été de juin, de juillet et d'août.
J'ai vu des soirs d'hiver posés comme un manteau.
J'ai vu des soirs d'été calmes et doux comme une tombée de
   paradis
Tout constellés d'étoiles.
J'ai vu ces coteaux de la Meuse et ces églises qui sont mes
   propres maisons,
Et Paris et Reims et Rouen et des cathédrales qui sont mes
   propres palais et mes propres châteaux.
Si beaux que je les garderai dans le ciel.
J'ai vu la capitale du royaume et Rome capitale de chrétienté.
J'ai entendu chanter la messe et les triomphantes vêpres.
Et j'ai vu ces plaines et ces vallonnements de France.

And comforting himself as if the good Lord were comforting
    him.
But let me tell you that those words of comfort which he says
    to himself
Come straight and properly from me.—

Nothing is so beautiful as a child going to sleep while he is
    saying his prayers, says God.
I tell you nothing is so beautiful in the world.—
And yet I have seen beautiful sights in the world.
And I know something about it. My creation is overflowing
    with beauty.
My creation overflows with marvels.
There are so many that you don't know where to put them.
I have seen millions and millions of stars rolling under my
    feet like the sands of the sea.
I have seen days as scorching as flames,
Summer days of June and July and August.
I have seen winter evenings spread out like a cloak.
I have seen summer evenings as calm and soft as something
    shed by Paradise,
All studded with stars.
I have seen those slopes of the Meuse and those churches
    which are my own houses,
And Paris and Reims and Rouen and cathedrals which are
    my own palaces and my own castles,
So beautiful that I am going to keep them in heaven.
I have seen the capital of the kingdom and Rome the capital
    of Christendom.
I have heard mass sung and triumphant vespers.
And I have seen the plains and vales of France,

Qui sont plus beaux que tout.

J'ai vu la profonde mer, et la forêt profonde, et le cœur profond de l'homme.

J'ai vu des cœurs dévorés d'amour

Pendant des vies entières,

Perdus de charité.

Brûlant comme des flammes. —

J'ai vu des martyrs flamber comme des torches

Se préparant ainsi les palmes toujours vertes.

Et j'ai vu perler sous les griffes de fer

Des gouttes de sang qui resplendissaient comme des diamants.

Et j'ai vu perler des larmes d'amour

Qui dureront plus longtemps que les étoiles du ciel.

Et j'ai vu des regards de prière, des regards de tendresse,

Perdus de charité

Qui brilleront éternellement dans les nuits et les nuits.

Et j'ai vu des vies tout entières de la naissance à la mort,

Du baptême au viatique,

Se dérouler comme un bel écheveau de laine.

Or je le dis, dit Dieu, je ne connais rien d'aussi beau dans
tout le monde

Qu'un petit enfant qui s'endort en faisant sa prière

Sous l'aile de son ange gardien

Et qui rit aux anges en commençant de s'endormir;

Et qui déjà mêle tout ça ensemble et qui n'y comprend plus
rien

Et qui fourre les paroles du *Notre Père* à tort et à travers
pêle-mêle dans les paroles du *Je vous salue Marie*

Pendant qu'un voile déjà descend sur ses paupières

Le voile de la nuit sur son regard et sur sa voix.

And they are more beautiful than anything.

I have seen the deep sea, and the deep forest, and the deep
  heart of man.

I have seen hearts devoured by love

During whole lifetimes

Lost in love

Burning like flames.—

I have seen martyrs blazing like torches,

Thus preparing for themselves palms everlastingly green.

And I have seen, beading under claws of iron,

Drops of blood which sparkled like diamonds.

And I have seen beading tears of love

Which will last longer than the stars in heaven.

And I have seen looks of prayer, looks of tenderness,

Lost in love,

Which will gleam for all eternity, nights and nights.

And I have seen whole lives from birth to death,

From baptism to viaticum,

Unrolling like a beautiful skein of wool.

But I tell you, says God, that I know of nothing so beautiful
  in the whole world

As a little child going to sleep while he is saying his prayers

Under the wing of his guardian angel

And laughs happily as he watches the angels and begins to
  go to sleep;

And is already mixing his prayers together and no longer
  knows what they are all about;

And sticks the words of *Our Father* among the words of *Hail,
  Mary*, all in a jumble,

While a veil is already coming down over his eyelids,

The veil of night over his gaze and over his voice.

J'ai vu les plus grands saints, dit Dieu. Eh bien je vous le dis

Je n'ai jamais rien vu de si drôle et par conséquent je ne
connais rien de si beau dans le monde

Que cet enfant qui s'endort en faisant sa prière

(Que ce petit être qui s'endort de confiance)

Et qui mélange son *Notre Père* avec son *Je vous salue Marie.*

Rien n'est aussi beau et c'est même un point

Où la Sainte Vierge est de mon avis —

Et je peux bien dire que c'est le seul point où nous soyons du
même avis. Car généralement nous sommes d'un avis
contraire.

Parce qu'elle est pour la miséricorde.

Et moi il faut bien que je sois pour la justice.

I have seen the greatest saints, says God. But I tell you
I have never seen anything so funny and I therefore know
   of nothing so beautiful in the world
As that child going to sleep while he says his prayers
(As that little creature going to sleep in all confidence)
And getting his *Our Father* mixed up with his *Hail, Mary.*
Nothing is so beautiful and it is even one point
On which the Blessed Virgin agrees with me—
And I can even say it is the only point on which we agree.
   Because as a rule we disagree,
She being for mercy,
Whereas I, of course, have to be for justice.

DIEU ET LA FRANCE

DIEU PARLE :

Nos Français — Ils sont mes témoins.
Préférés.
Ce sont eux qui marchent le plus tout seuls.
Ce sont eux qui marchent le plus eux-mêmes.
Entre tous ils sont libres et entre tous ils sont gratuits.
Ils n'ont pas besoin qu'on leur explique vingt fois la même
   chose.
Avant qu'on ait fini de parler, ils sont partis.
Peuple intelligent,
Avant qu'on ait fini de parler, ils ont compris.
Peuple laborieux,
Avant qu'on ait fini de parler, l'œuvre est faite.
Peuple militaire,
Avant qu'on ait fini de parler, la bataille est donnée. —
C'est embêtant, dit Dieu. Quand il n'y aura plus ces Français,
Il y a des choses que je fais, il n'y aura plus personne pour
   les comprendre.
Peuple, les peuples de la terre te disent léger
Parce que tu es un peuple prompt.
Les peuples pharisiens te disent léger
Parce que tu es un peuple vite.

GOD AND FRANCE

GOD SPEAKS:

Our Frenchmen—They are my favorite witnesses.
They go ahead by themselves more than the others.
They go ahead and are themselves more than the others.
Among all men they are free and among all gratuitous.
You don't have to tell them the same thing twenty times over.
Before you are through talking, they are on their way.
Intelligent people.
Before you are through talking, they have understood.
Hard working people,
Before you are through talking, the work is done.
Military people,
Before you are through talking, the battle is begun—
It is very annoying, says God. When there are no more
    Frenchmen,
Well, there are things that I do, and nobody will be there to
    understand them.
French people, the peoples of the earth call you lightheaded
Because you are quick.
The Pharisee peoples call you lightheaded
Because you are a quick people.

Tu es arrivé avant que les autres soient partis.

Mais moi je t'ai pesé, dit Dieu, et je ne t'ai point trouvé léger.

O peuple inventeur de la cathédrale, je ne t'ai point trouvé
léger en foi.

O peuple inventeur de la croisade je ne t'ai point trouvé léger
en charité.

Quant à l'espérance, il vaut mieux ne pas en parler, il n'y en
a que pour eux.

Tels sont nos Français, dit Dieu. Ils ne sont pas sans défauts.
Il s'en faut. Ils ont même beaucoup de défauts.

Ils ont plus de défauts que les autres.

Mais avec tous leurs défauts je les aime encore mieux que tous
les autres avec censément moins de défauts,

Je les aime comme ils sont. Il n'y a que moi, dit Dieu, qui
suis sans défaut. Mon fils et moi. —

Nos Français sont comme tout le monde, dit Dieu, peu de
saints, beaucoup de pécheurs.

Un saint, trois pécheurs. Et trente pécheurs. Et trois cents
pécheurs. Et plus.

Mais j'aime mieux un saint qui a des défauts qu'un pécheur
qui n'en a pas. Non, je veux dire:

J'aime mieux un saint qui a des défauts qu'un neutre qui n'en
a pas.

Je suis ainsi. *Un homme avait deux fils.*

Or ces Français, comme ils sont, ce sont mes meilleurs servi-
teurs.

Ils ont été, ils seront toujours mes meilleurs soldats dans la
croisade.

Or il y aura toujours la croisade.

Enfin ils me plaisent. C'est tout dire.

You reach the goal before the others have started.

But I have weighed you, says God, and I have not found you wanting.

O people who invented the cathedral, I have not found you wanting in faith.

O people who invented the crusade, I have not found you wanting in charity.

As for hope, it might be better not to mention that, because they have taken all of it.

Such are our Frenchmen, says God. They are not without their faults. Far from it. You might even say they have a great many faults.

They have more faults than other people.

But with all their faults I love them still more than I do all the others who, supposedly, have fewer faults.

I love them as they are. I alone have no faults, says God. My son and I.

Our Frenchmen are like everyone else, says God. Few saints, many sinners.

One saint, three sinners. And thirty sinners. And three hundred sinners. And more.

But I prefer a saint who has his faults to a sinner who has none. No, what I mean is this:

I prefer a saint who has his faults to a neutral who has none.

That is the way I am. *A certain man had two sons.*

Now those Frenchmen, just as they are, are my best servants.

They have been and always will be my best soldiers in the crusade.

And there will always be a crusade.

In short, they please me. And that is all there is about it.

LA PASSION DE NOTRE DAME

C'était de leur faute. Ça devait être de leur faute.
Ils en avaient toujours été trop fiers.
Joseph et elle ils en étaient trop fiers.
Ça devait mal finir.
Il ne faut pas être fier comme ça.
Il ne faut pas se glorifier.

En avaient-ils eu du contentement.
Le jour que ce vieillard Siméon
Avait entonné ce cantique au Seigneur.
Qui sera chanté dans les siècles des siècles.
Ainsi soit-il.
Et il y avait aussi cette vieille bonne femme dans le temple.

En avaient-ils été fiers.
Trop fiers.

Et cette fois aussi.
Cette fois qu'il brilla parmi les docteurs.
Ils en avaient eu d'abord un saisissement.

THE PASSION OF OUR LADY

It was their fault. It must have been their fault.
They had always been too proud of him.
Joseph and she, they had been too proud of him.
It was bound to end badly.
You mustn't be so proud.
You mustn't be as proud as that.—

Weren't they pleased
On the day when that old fellow Simeon
Sang that hymn to the Lord,
Which will be sung forever and ever.
Amen.
And then there was that old woman in the temple.

Weren't they proud!
Too proud.

And that other time too.
The time when he shone among the doctors.
At first they got quite a jolt,

En rentrant à la maison.
Il n'était pas là.
Tout d'un coup il n'était pas là.
Ils croyaient l'avoir oublié quelque part.
Elle en était encore toute saisie.
Ils croyaient l'avoir perdu. —
C'est pas rigolo. Elle en tremblait encore.
C'était pas ordinaire.
Ce n'est pas une aventure ordinaire de perdre un garçon de
    douze ans.
Un grand garçon de douze ans.

Heureusement ils l'avaient retrouvé dans le temple au milieu
    des docteurs.
Assis au milieu des docteurs.
Les docteurs l'écoutaient religieusement.
Il enseignait, à douze ans il enseignait au milieu des docteurs.
Comme ils en avaient été fiers.
Trop fiers.

Il aurait dû tout de même se méfier ce jour-là.
Il était vraiment trop brillant, il brillait trop, il rayonnait
    trop parmi les docteurs.
Pour les docteurs.
Il était trop grand parmi les docteurs.
Pour les docteurs.
Il avait fait voir trop visiblement.
Il avait trop laissé voir.
Il avait trop manifesté qu'il était Dieu.
Les docteurs n'aiment pas ça.

When they came home
And he wasn't with them,
All of a sudden he wasn't with them.
They thought they had forgotten him somewhere.
Mary was all taken aback.
They thought they had lost him.—
That was no joke. It made her tremble.
It wasn't something that happened every day
To lose a twelve year old boy.
A big twelve year old boy.

Fortunately they found him in the temple in the midst of the
    doctors.
Sitting in the midst of the doctors.
And the doctors listening religiously.
He was teaching, at the age of twelve, he was teaching in the
    midst of the doctors.
How proud they had felt.
Too proud.

Just the same, he ought to have been careful, that day.
He had really been too brilliant, he shone too much in the
    midst of the doctors.
Too much for the doctors.
He was too great among the doctors.
For the doctors.
He had let it be seen too clearly.
He had let it be seen too much.
He had made it known too manifestly that he was God.
Doctors don't like that.

Il aurait dû se méfier. Ces gens-là ont de la mémoire.
C'est même pour cela qu'ils sont docteurs.
Il les avait sûrement blessés ce jour-là.
Les docteurs ont une bonne mémoire.
Les docteurs ont la mémoire longue.

Il aurait dû se méfier. Ces gens-là ont la mémoire longue.
Et puis ils se tiennent entre eux.
Ils se soutiennent.
Les docteurs ont la mémoire longue.
Il les avait sûrement blessés ce jour-là.
A douze ans.
Et à trente-trois ans ils le rattrapaient.
Et cette fois ils ne le rateraient pas.
C'était la mort.
Ils l'avaient.
Ils avaient sa peau.
A trente-trois ans ils l'avaient rattrapé.
Les docteurs ont la mémoire longue. —

Il avait été un bon fils pour ses père et mère.
Jusqu'au jour où il avait commencé sa mission. —
Il était généralement aimé.
Tout le monde l'aimait bien.
Jusqu'au jour où il avait commencé sa mission.
Les camarades, les amis, les compagnons, les autorités,
Les citoyens,
Les père et mère

He ought to have been more careful. People like that have
  good memories.
It is even because they have such good memories that they
  are doctors.
He surely hurt their feelings that day.
And doctors have a good memory.
Doctors have a memory that goes way back.

He ought to have been more careful. Those people have a
  memory that goes back a good deal.
And then they always stick together.
They uphold each other.
Doctors have a memory that goes way back.
He surely hurt their feelings that day.
When he was twelve.
And when he was thirty-three, they got him.
And this time they wouldn't let him off.
It meant death.
They had him.
They got him.
When he was thirty-three they caught him.
Doctors have a memory that goes way back.—

He had been a good son to his father and mother.
Until the day when he began his mission.—
He was generally liked.
Everybody liked him.
Until the day when he began his mission.
His comrades, his friends, his companions, the authorities,
The citizens,
His father and mother,

Trouvaient cela très bien.
Jusqu'au jour où il avait commencé sa mission. —

Les autorités trouvaient cela très bien.
Jusqu'au jour où il avait commencé sa mission.
Les autorités trouvaient qu'il était un homme d'ordre.
Un jeune homme posé.
Un jeune homme tranquille.
Un jeune homme rangé.
Commode à gouverner.
Et qui rendait à César ce qui est à César.
Jusqu'au jour où il avait commencé le désordre.
Introduit le désordre.
Le plus grand désordre qu'il y ait eu dans le monde.
Qu'il y ait jamais eu dans le monde.
Le plus grand ordre qu'il y ait eu dans le monde.
Le seul ordre.
Qu'il y ait jamais eu dans le monde. —

Il était un bon fils pour ses père et mère.
Un bon fils pour sa mère Marie.
Et ses père et mère trouvaient cela très bien.
Sa mère Marie trouvait cela très bien.
Elle était heureuse, elle était fière d'avoir un tel fils.
D'être la mère d'un pareil fils. —
Elle s'en glorifiait peut-être en elle-même et elle glorifiait
    Dieu.
Magnificat anima mea.
Dominum.
Et exultavit spiritus meus.
Magnificat. Magnificat.

They all thought what he did was all right.
Until the day when he began his mission.—

The authorities thought what he did was all right.
Until the day when he began his mission.
The authorities considered he was a man of order.
A serious young man.
A quiet young man.
A young man with good habits.
Easy to govern.
Giving back to Caesar what was Caesar's.
Until the day when he had begun disorder.
Introduced disorder.
The greatest disorder in the world.
The greatest there ever was in the world.
The greatest order there had been in the world.
The only order.
There had ever been in the world.—

He was a good son to his father and mother.
He was a good son to his mother Mary.
And his father and mother thought everything was all right.
His mother Mary thought it was all right.
She was happy, she was proud of having such a son.
Of being the mother of such a son.—
And she gloried perhaps a little in herself, and she magnified
    God.
Magnificat anima mea.
Dominum.
Et exultavit spiritus meus.
Magnificat. Magnificat.

Jusqu'au jour où il avait commencé sa mission. —
Elle ne magnifiait peut-être plus.
Depuis trois jours elle pleurait.
Elle pleurait, elle pleurait.
Comme aucune femme n'a jamais pleuré. —
Jamais un garçon n'avait coûté autant de larmes à sa mère.
Jamais un garçon n'avait autant fait pleurer sa mère.
Voilà ce qu'il avait rapporté à sa mère.
Depuis qu'il avait commencé sa mission. —

Depuis trois jours elle errait, elle suivait.
Elle suivait le cortège.
Elle suivait les événements.
Elle suivait comme à un enterrement.
Mais c'était l'enterrement d'un vivant. —
Elle suivait comme une suivante.
Comme une servante.
Comme une pleureuse des Romains. —
Comme si ça avait été son métier.
De pleurer. —
Voilà ce qu'il avait fait de sa mère.
Depuis qu'il avait commencé sa mission. —
On la voyait partout.
Dans le cortège mais un peu en dehors du cortège.
Sous les portiques, sous les arcades, dans les courants d'air.
Dans les temples, dans les palais.
Dans les rues.
Dans les cours et dans les arrière-cours.
Et elle était montée aussi sur le Calvaire.
Elle aussi elle avait gravi le Calvaire.
Qui est une montagne escarpée.

Until the day when he had begun his mission.—
Perhaps she no longer said *Magnificat* then.
For the last three days she wept.
She wept and wept
As no other woman has ever wept.—
No boy had ever cost his mother so many tears.
No boy had ever made his mother weep as much.
And that is what he had done to his mother
Since he had begun his mission.—

For the past three days she had been wandering, and follow-
    ing.
She followed the people.
She followed the events.
She seemed to be following a funeral.
But it was a living man's funeral.—
She followed like a follower.
Like a servant.
Like a weeper at a Roman funeral.—
As if it had been her only occupation.
To weep.—
That is what he had done to his mother.
Since the day when he had begun his mission.—
You saw her everywhere.
With the people and a little apart from the people.
Under the porticoes, under the arcades, in drafty places.
In the temples, in the palaces.
In the streets.
In the yards and in the back-yards.
And she had also gone up to Calvary.
She too had climbed up Calvary.
A very steep hill.

Et elle ne sentait seulement pas qu'elle marchait.

Elle ne sentait seulement pas ses pieds qui la portaient. —

Elle aussi elle avait gravi son calvaire.

Elle aussi elle avait monté, monté

Dans la cohue, un peu en arrière. —

Elle pleurait, elle pleurait sous un grand voile de lin.

Un grand voile bleu.

Un peu passé. —

Elle pleurait comme jamais il ne sera donné;

Comme jamais il ne sera demandé

A une femme de pleurer sur terre.

Eternellement jamais. —

Ce qu'il y a de curieux c'est que tout le monde la respectait.

Les gens respectent beaucoup les parents des condamnés.

Ils disaient même: *la pauvre femme.*

Et en même temps ils tapaient sur son fils.

Parce que l'homme est comme ça. —

Le monde est comme ça.

Les hommes sont comme ils sont et on ne pourra jamais les
changer.

Elle ne savait pas qu'au contraire il était venu changer
l'homme.

Qu'il était venu changer le monde.

Elle suivait, elle pleurait.

Et en même temps ils tapaient sur son garçon. —

Elle suivait, elle pleurait.

Tout le monde la respectait.

Tout le monde la plaignait.

On disait *la pauvre femme.*

C'est que tous ces gens n'étaient peut-être pas méchants.

Ils n'étaient pas méchants au fond.

And she did not even feel that she was walking.
She did not even feel that her feet were carrying her.—
She too had gone up *her* Calvary.
She too had gone up and up
In the general confusion, lagging a little behind . . .
She wept and wept under a big linen veil.
A big blue veil.
A little faded.—
She wept as it will never be granted to a woman to weep.
As it will never be asked
Of a woman to weep on this earth.
Never at any time.—
What was very strange was that everyone respected her.
People greatly respect the parents of the condemned.
They even said: *Poor woman.*
And at the same time they struck at her son.
Because man is like that.—
The world is like that.
Men are what they are and you never can change them.
She did not know that, on the contrary, he had come to change
   man.
That he had come to change the world.
She followed and wept.
And at the same time they were beating her boy.—
She followed and wept.
Everybody respected her.
Everybody pitied her.
They said: *Poor woman.*
Because they weren't perhaps really bad.
They weren't bad at heart.

Ils accomplissaient les Ecritures. —

Tout le monde honorait, respectait, admirait sa douleur.

On ne l'écartait, on ne la repoussait que modérément.

Avec des attentions particulières.

Parce qu'elle était la mère du condamné.

On pensait: c'est la famille du condamné.

On le disait même à voix basse.

On se le disait, entre soi,

Avec une secrète admiration. —

Elle suivait, elle pleurait, elle ne comprenait pas très bien.

Mais elle comprenait très bien que le gouvernement était
contre son garçon.

Ce qui est une mauvaise affaire. —

Tous les gouvernements s'étaient mis d'accord contre lui.

Le gouvernement des Juifs et le gouvernement des Romains.

Le gouvernement des juges et le gouvernement des prêtres.

Le gouvernement des soldats et le gouvernement des curés.

Il n'en réchapperait sûrement pas.

Certainement pas. —

Ce qui était curieux c'est que la dérision était toute sur lui.

Et qu'il n'y avait aucune dérision sur elle. —

On n'avait que du respect pour elle.

Pour sa douleur. —

On ne lui disait pas des sottises.

Au contraire.

Les gens ne la regardaient même pas trop.

Afin de mieux la respecter. —

Elle aussi elle était montée.

They fulfilled the Scriptures.—

They honored, respected and admired her grief.

They didn't make her go away, they pushed her back only a
  little

With special attentions

Because she was the mother of the condemned.

They thought: It's the family of the condemned.

They even said so in a low voice.

They said it among themselves

With a secret admiration.—

She followed and wept, and didn't understand very well.

But she understood quite well that the government was against
  her boy.

And that is a very bad business.—

She understood that all the governments were together against
  her boy.

The government of the Jews and the government of the
  Romans.

The government of judges and the government of priests.

The government of soldiers and the government of parsons.

He could never gét out of it.

Certainly not.—

What was strange was that all derision was heaped on him.

Not on her at all.—

There was only respect for her.

For her grief.—

They didn't insult her.

On the contrary.

People even refrained from looking at her too much.

All the more to respect her.

So she too had gone up.

Montée avec tout le monde.

Jusqu'au faîte.

Sans même s'en apercevoir.

Ses jambes la portaient sans même s'en apercevoir.

Elle aussi elle avait fait son chemin de croix.

Les quatorze stations.

Au fait était-ce bien quatorze stations.

Y avait-il bien quatorze stations. —

Elle ne savait plus au juste.

Elle ne se rappelait plus.

Pourtant elle les avait faites.

Elle en était sûre.

Mais on peut se tromper.

Dans ces moments-là la tête se trouble. —

Tout le monde était contre lui.

Tout le monde voulait sa mort.

C'est curieux.

Des mondes qui d'habitude n'étaient pas ensemble.

Le gouvernement et le peuple. —

C'était jouer de malheur.

Quand on a l'un pour soi, l'autre contre soi quelquefois on en
    réchappe.

On s'en tire. —

Mais il n'en réchapperait pas.

Sûrement il n'en réchapperait pas.

Quand on a tout le monde contre soi.

Qu'est-ce qu'il avait donc fait à tout le monde.

Je vais vous le dire :

Il avait sauvé le monde.

Gone up with everybody else.
Up to the very top of the hill.
Without even being aware of it.
Her legs had carried her and she did not even know it.
She too had made the Way of the Cross.
The fourteen stations of the Way of the Cross.
Were there fourteen stations?
Were there really fourteen stations?—
She didn't know for sure.
She couldn't remember.
Yet she had not missed one.
She was sure of that.
But you can always make a mistake.
In moments like that your head swims. . . .
Everybody was against him.
Everybody wanted him to die.
It is strange.
People who are not usually together.
The government and the people.—
That was awful luck.
When you have someone for you and someone against you,
    sometimes you can get out of it.
You can scramble out of it.
But he wouldn't.
Certainly he wouldn't.
When you have everyone against you.
But what had he done to everyone?

I'll tell you.
He had saved the world.

VISION DE PRIERE

DIEU PARLE :

Je suis leur père, dit Dieu. *Notre Père, qui êtes aux Cieux.*
  Mon fils le leur a assez dit, que je suis leur père.
Je suis leur juge. Mon fils le leur a dit. Je suis aussi leur père.
Je suis surtout leur père.
Enfin je suis leur père. Celui qui est père est surtout père.
  Notre Père qui êtes aux Cieux. Celui qui a été une fois
  père ne peut plus être que père.
Ils sont les frères de mon fils; ils sont mes enfants; je suis leur
  père.
Notre Père qui êtes aux Cieux, mon fils leur a enseigné cette
  prière. *Sic ergo vos orabitis. Vous prierez donc ainsi.*
Notre Père qui êtes aux Cieux, il a bien su ce qu'il faisait ce
  jour-là, mon fils qui les aimait tant.
Qui a vécu parmi eux, qui était un comme eux.
Qui allait comme eux, qui parlait comme eux, qui vivait
  comme eux.
Qui souffrait.
Qui souffrit comme eux, qui mourut comme eux.
Et qui les aime tant les ayant connus.

A VISION OF PRAYER

GOD SPEAKS:

I am their father, says God. *Our Father who art in Heaven.*
  My son told them often enough that I was their father.
I am their judge. My son told them so. I am also their father.
I am especially their father.
Well, I am their father. He who is a father is above all a
  father. *Our Father who art in Heaven.* He who has once
  been a father can be nothing else but a father.
They are my son's brothers; they are my children; I am their
  father.
Our Father who art in Heaven, my son taught them that
  prayer. *Sic ergo vos orabitis.* After this manner therefore
  pray ye.
Our Father who art in Heaven, he knew very well what he
  was doing that day, my son who loved them so.
Who lived among them, who was like one of them.
Who went as they did, who spoke as they did, who lived as
  they did.
Who suffered.
Who suffered as they did, who died as they did.
And who loved them so, having known them.

Qui a rapporté dans le ciel un certain goût de l'homme, un
   certain goût de la terre.

Mon fils qui les a tant aimés, qui les aime éternellement dans
   le ciel.

Il a bien su ce qu'il faisait ce jour-là, mon fils qui les aime
   tant,

Quand il a mis cette barrière entre eux et moi, *Notre Père
   qui êtes aux Cieux,* ces trois ou quatre mots.

Cette barrière que ma colère et peut-être ma justice ne fran-
   chira jamais.

Heureux celui qui s'endort sous la protection de l'avancée de
   ces trois ou quatre mots.

Ces mots qui marchent devant toute prière comme les mains
   du suppliant marchent devant sa face,

Comme les deux mains jointes du suppliant s'avancent devant
   sa face et les larmes de sa face.

Ces trois ou quatre mots qui me vainquent, moi l'invincible.

Et qu'ils font marcher devant leur détresse comme deux mains
   jointes invincibles.

Ces trois ou quatre mots qui s'avancent comme un bel éperon
   devant un pauvre navire,

Et qui fendent le flot de ma colère.

Et quand l'éperon est passé, le navire passe, et toute la flotte
   derrière.

Actuellement, dit Dieu, c'est ainsi que je les vois;

Et pour mon éternité, éternellement, dit Dieu.

Par cette invention de mon Fils éternellement c'est ainsi qu'il
   faut que je les voie.

(Et qu'il faut que je les juge. Comment voulez-vous, à présent, que je les juge.

Après cela).

Who brought back to heaven a certain taste for man, a certain
  taste for the earth.
My son who loved them so, who loves them eternally in
  heaven.
He knew very well what he was doing that day, my son who
  loved them so.
When he put that barrier between them and me, *Our Father
  who art in Heaven,* those three or four words.
That barrier which my anger and perhaps my justice will
  never pass.
Blessed is the man who goes to sleep under the protection of
  that outpost, the outpost of those three or four words.
Those words that move ahead of every prayer like the hands
  of the suppliant in front of his face.
Like the two joined hands of the suppliant advancing before
  his face and the tears of his face.
Those three or four words that conquer me, the uncon-
  querable.
And which they cause to go before their distress like two
  joined and invincible hands.
Those three or four words which move forward like a beauti-
  ful cutwater fronting a lowly ship.
Cutting the flood of my anger.
And when the cutwater has passed, the ship passes, and back
  of them the whole fleet.
That, actually, is the way I see them, says God;
During my eternity, eternally, says God.
Because of that invention of my Son's, thus must I eternally
  see them.
(And judge them. How do you expect me to judge them now.
After that.)

Notre Père qui êtes aux Cieux, mon fils a très bien su s'y
    prendre.

Pour lier les bras de ma justice et pour délier les bras de
    ma miséricorde.

(Je ne parle pas de ma colère, qui n'a jamais été que ma
    justice.

Et quelquefois ma charité).

Et à présent il faut que je les juge comme un père. Pour ce
    que ça peut juger, un père! *Un homme avait deux fils.*

Pour ce que c'est capable de juger. *Un homme avait deux fils.*
    On sait assez comment un père juge. Il y en a un exemple
    connu.

On sait assez comment le père a jugé le fils qui était parti et
    qui est revenu.

C'est encore le père qui pleurait le plus.

Voilà ce que mon fils leur a conté. Mon fils leur a livré

Le secret du jugement même.

Et à présent voici comme ils me paraissent; voici comme je les
    vois;

Voici comme je suis forcé de les voir.

De même que le sillage d'un beau vaisseau va en s'élargissant
    jusqu'à disparaître et se perdre,

Mais commence par une pointe, qui est la pointe même du
    vaisseau.

Ainsi le sillage immense des pécheurs s'élargit jusqu'à dis-
    paraître et se perdre,

Mais il commence par une pointe, et c'est cette pointe qui
    vient vers moi,

Qui est tournée vers moi.

Il commence par une pointe, qui est la pointe même du
    vaisseau.

Our Father who art in Heaven, my son knew exactly what
  to do

In order to tie the arms of my justice and untie the arms of
  my mercy.

(I do not mention my anger, which has never been anything
  but my justice.

And sometimes my charity.)

And now I must judge them like a father. As if a father were
  any good as a judge. *A certain man had two sons.*

As if he were capable of judging. *A certain man had two
  sons.* We know well enough how a father judges. There is
  a famous example of that.

We know well enough how the father judged the son who
  had gone away and came back.

The father wept even more than the son.

That is the story my son has been telling them. My son gave
  them

The secret of judgement itself.

And now this is how they seem to me; this is how I see them;

This is how I am obliged to see them.

Just as the wake of a beautiful ship grows wider and wider
  until it disappears and loses itself,

But begins with a point, which is the point of the ship itself.

So the huge wake of sinners grows wider and wider until
  it disappears and loses itself

But it begins with a point, which is the point of the ship itself,
  and it is that point which comes towards me,

Which is turned towards me.

It begins with a point, which is the point of the ship itself.

Et le vaisseau est mon propre fils, chargé de tous les péchés du monde.

Et la pointe du vaisseau ce sont les deux mains jointes de mon fils.

Et devant le regard de ma colère et devant le regard de ma justice

Ils se sont tous dérobés derrière lui.

Et tout cet immense cortège des prières, tout ce sillage immense s'élargit jusqu'à disparaître et se perdre.

Mais il commence par une pointe et c'est cette pointe qui est tournée vers moi.

Qui s'avance vers moi.

Et cette pointe ce sont ces trois ou quatre mots: *Notre Père qui êtes aux Cieux;* mon fils en vérité savait ce qu'il faisait.

Et toute prière monte vers moi dérobée derrière ces trois ou quatre mots. —

Notre Père qui êtes aux Cieux, — et derrière (ces mots) s'élargit jusqu'à disparaître et se perdre

Le sillage des prières innombrables

Comme elles sont prononcées dans leur texte dans les jours innombrables

Par les hommes innombrables,

(Par les simples hommes, ses frères).

Prières du matin, prières du soir;

(Prières prononcées toutes les autres fois),

Tant d'autres fois dans les innombrables jours;

Prières du midi et de toute la journée;

Prières des moines pour toutes les heures du jour,

Et pour les heures de la nuit;

Prières des laïcs et prières des clercs

Comme elles furent prononcées d'innombrables fois

And the ship is my own son, laden with all the sins of the
world.
And the point of the ship is the two joined hands of my son.
And before the look of my anger and the look of my justice
They have all hidden behind him.
And all of that huge cortège of prayers, all of that huge
wake grows wider and wider until it disappears and loses
itself.
But it begins with a point and it is that point which is turned
towards me.
Which advances towards me.
And that point is those three or four words: *Our Father who
art in Heaven;* verily my son knew what he was doing.
And every prayer comes up to me hidden behind those three
or four words.—
Our Father who art in Heaven.—And behind (these words)
widens until it disappears and loses itself
The wake of innumerable prayers
As they are spoken in their text for innumerable days
By innumerable men,
(By simple men, his brothers).
Morning prayers, evening prayers;
(Prayers said on all other occasions);
On so many other occasions during innumerable days;
Prayers for noon and for the whole day;
Prayers of monks for all hours of the day,
And for the hours of the night;
Laymen's prayers and clerics' prayers
As they were said innumerable times

Dans les innombrables jours.

(Il parlait comme eux, il parlait avec eux, il parlait l'un
d'eux).

Toute cette immense flotte de prières chargée des péchés du
monde,

Toute cette immense flotte de prières et de pénitences
m'attaque

Ayant l'éperon que vous savez,

S'avance vers moi ayant l'éperon que vous savez.

C'est une flotte de charge, *classis oneraria.*

Et c'est une flotte de ligne,

Une flotte de combat.

Comme une belle flotte antique, comme une flotte de trirèmes

Qui s'avancerait à l'attaque du roi.

Et moi que voulez-vous que je fasse: je suis attaqué.

Et dans cette flotte, dans cette innombrable flotte,

Chaque *Pater* est comme un vaisseau de haut bord

Qui a lui-même son propre éperon, *Notre Père qui êtes aux
Cieux,*

Tourné vers moi, et qui s'avance derrière ce propre éperon.

Notre Père qui êtes aux Cieux, ce n'est pas malin. Evidemment
quand un homme a dit ça, il peut se cacher derrière,

Quand il a prononcé ces trois ou quatre mots.

Et derrière ces beaux vaisseaux de haut bord les *Ave Maria*

S'avancent comme des galères innocentes, comme de virgi-
nales birèmes.

Comme des vaisseaux plats, qui ne blessent point l'humilité
de la mer.

Qui ne blessent point la règle, qui suivent, humbles et fidèles
et soumis au ras de l'eau.

Notre Père qui êtes aux Cieux. Evidemment quand un homme
a commencé comme ça.

For innumerable days.

(He spoke like them, he spoke with them, he spoke as one of
    them.)

All of that huge fleet of prayers laden with the sins of the
    world.

All of that huge fleet of prayers and penances attacks me

Having the spear you wot of,

Advances towards me having the spear you wot of.

It is a fleet of freighters, *classis oneraria.*

And a fleet of the line,

A combat fleet.

Like a beautiful fleet of yore, like a fleet of triremes

Advancing to attack the king.

And what do you expect me to do: I am attacked

And in that fleet, in that innumerable fleet

Each *Our Father* is like a high riding ship

Having itself its own spear, *Our Father who art in Heaven*

Turned towards me, and coming behind this selfsame spear.

Our Father who art in Heaven, not so smart after all. Of
    course, when a man says that, he can get behind what he
    has said.

When he has said those three or four words.

And behind those beautiful high riding ships, the *Hail Marys*

Advance like innocent galleys, like virginal biremes.

Like flat-bottomed boats which do not offend the humility of
    the sea.

Which do not offend the rule, which follow, humble and faith-
    ful in their submissiveness on the surface of the water.

Our Father who art in Heaven. Of course when a man begins
    like that.

Quand il m'a dit ces trois ou quatre mots,

Quand il a commencé par faire marcher devant lui ces trois
ou quatre mots.

Après il peut continuer, il peut me dire ce qu'il voudra.

Vous comprenez, moi, je suis désarmé.

Et mon fils le savait bien.

Qui a tant aimé ces hommes,

Qui avait pris goût à eux, et à la terre, et à tout ce qui s'ensuit.

Et dans cette flotte innombrable je distingue nettement trois
grandes flottes innombrables.

(Je suis Dieu, je vois clair).

Et voici ce que je vois dans cet immense sillage qui commence
par cette pointe et qui de proche en proche peu à peu se
perd à l'horizon de mon regard.

Ils sont tous l'un derrière l'autre, même ceux qui débordent
le sillage

Vers ma main gauche et vers ma main droite.

En tête marche la flotte innombrable des *Pater*

Fendant et bravant le flot de ma colère,

Puissamment assis sur leurs trois rangs de rames.

(Voilà comme je suis attaqué. Je vous le demande. Est-ce
juste?)

(Non, ce n'est point juste, car tout ceci est du règne de ma
Miséricorde)

Et tous ces pécheurs et tous ces saints ensemble marchent
derrière mon fils

Et derrière les mains jointes de mon fils.

When he says those three or four words to me.

When he begins by making those three or four words move
ahead of him.

After that he can go on, he can tell me what he pleases.

Because, you understand, I am disarmed.

And my son knew it well.

My son who loved those men so very much.

Who had acquired a taste for them, and for the earth, and all
that.

And in this innumerable fleet I clearly distinguish three great
innumerable fleets.

(I am God, I see well).

And this is what I see in that huge wake which begins with
that point and which little by little loses itself on the
horizon of my gaze.

They are all one behind the other, even those which are outside the wake,

Towards my left hand and towards my right hand.

At the head of all of them comes the innumerable fleet of
Our Fathers

Cutting and defying the flood of my anger.

Powerfully seated on three rows of oars.

(That is the way I am attacked. I ask you. Is it fair? Is it
just?)

(No, it is not just, because all this has to do with the reign
of my Mercy)

So, all these sinners and all these saints, walking together
behind my son.

And behind the joined hands of my son,

Et eux-mêmes ont les mains jointes comme s'ils fussent mon
 fils.

Enfin mes fils. Enfin chacun un fils comme mon fils.

En tête marche la lourde flotte des *Pater* et c'est une flotte
 innombrable.

C'est dans cette formation qu'ils m'attaquent. Je pense que
 vous m'avez compris.

*Le royaume du ciel souffre la force, et les hommes de force
 le prendront de force.* Ils le savent bien. Mon fils leur a tout
 dit. *Regnum cœli*, le royaume du ciel. Ou *regnum cœlorum*,
 le royaume des cieux.

Regnum cœli vim patitur. Et violenti rapient illud. Ou *rapiunt.*
 Le royaume du ciel souffre la violence. Et les violents le
 violent. Ou le violeront.

Comment voulez-vous que je me défende? Mon fils leur a tout
 dit. Et non seulement cela. Mais dans le temps il s'est mis
 à leur tête. Et ils sont comme une grande flotte antique,
 comme une flotte innombrable qui s'attaquerait au grand
 roi. —

Du haut de mon promontoire,
Du promontoire de ma justice,
Et du siège de ma colère,
Et de la chaire de ma jurisprudence,
In *cathedra jurisprudentiae,*
Du trône de mon éternelle grandeur
Je vois monter vers moi, du fond de l'horizon je vois venir
Cette flotte qui m'assaille,
La triangulaire flotte,
Me présentant cette pointe que vous savez. —

And they themselves with joined hands as if they were my
son.

Well then, my sons. Well then each one a son like my son.

First comes the heavy fleet of *Our Fathers*, an innumerable
fleet.

And in that formation they attack me. I suppose you have
understood.

*The kingdom of heaven suffereth violence, and the violent
take it by force.* They know it well. My son told them
everything. *Regnum cœli*, the kingdom of heaven. Or
regnum cœlorum, the kingdom of heavens.

Regnum cœli vim patitur. Et violenti rapient illud. Or
rapiunt. The kingdom of heaven suffereth violence. And
the violent take it by force. Or will take it by force.

How do you expect me to defend myself? My son told them
everything. And not only did he do that. But he put himself at their head. And they are like a great fleet of yore,
like an innumerable fleet attacking the great king.—

From the high point of my promontory,
The promontory of my justice,
And from the seat of my anger,
And from the chair of my jurisprudence,
In cathedra jurisprudentiae,
From the throne of my eternal greatness
I see coming up towards me, from the far horizon I see com-
ing
This fleet which attacks me,
The triangular fleet,
Pointing towards me the spear you wot of.—

Et dans cette flotte innombrable je découvre trois flottes également innombrables.

Et la première est devant, pour m'attaquer plus durement.
C'est la flotte de haut bord,

Les navires à la puissante carène,

Cuirassés comme des hoplites,

C'est-à-dire comme des soldats pesamment armés.

Et ils se meuvent invinciblement portés sur leurs trois rangs
de rames.

Et le premier rang de rames est:
Que votre nom soit sanctifié,
Le vôtre;

Et le deuxième rang de rames est:
Que votre règne arrive,
Le vôtre;

Et le troisième rang de rames est la parole entre toutes
insurmontable:
Que votre volonté soit faite sur la terre comme au ciel,
La vôtre.
Sanctificetur nomen
Tuum.
Adveniat regnum
Tuum.
Fiat voluntas
Tua
Sicut in cœlo et in terra.

Et telle est la flotte des *Pater*, solide et plus innombrable que
les étoiles du ciel. Et derrière je vois la deuxième flotte, et

And in that innumerable fleet I discover three fleets equally
   innumerable.

And the first is in front, to attack me with greater vigor. The
   high riding fleet,

The ships of powerful hull,

Armored like hoplites,

That is, like soldiers heavily armed.

And they move invincibly ahead, borne on their triple rows
   of oars.

And the first row of oars is:

Hallowed be thy name,

Thy name;

And the second row of oars is:

Thy kingdom come

Thy kingdom;

And the third row of oars is the word insurmountable among
   all words,

Thy will be done on earth as it is in heaven,

Thy will.

Sanctificetur nomen

Tuum.

Adveniat regnum

Tuum.

Fiat voluntas

Tua

Sicut in cœlo et in terra.

And such is the fleet of *Our Fathers*, stalwart and more innumerable than the stars in heaven. And behind it I see

c'est une flotte innombrable, car c'est la flotte aux blanches
voiles, l'innombrable flotte des *Ave Maria.*
Et c'est une flotte de birèmes. Et le premier rang de rames est:
Ave Maria, gratia plena;

Et le deuxième rang de rames est;
Sancta Maria, mater Dei.

Et tous ces *Ave Maria,* et toutes ces prières de la Vierge et le
noble *Salve Regina* sont de blanches caravelles, humble-
ment couchées sous leurs voiles au ras de l'eau; comme de
blanches colombes que l'on prendrait dans la main.
Or ces douces colombes sous leurs ailes,
Ces blanches colombes familières, ces colombes dans la main,
Ces humbles colombes couchées au ras de la main,
Ces colombes accoutumées à la main,
Ces caravelles vêtues de voilures
De tous les vaisseaux ce sont les plus opportunes,
C'est-à-dire celles qui se présentent le plus directement devant
le port.

Telle est la deuxième flotte, ce sont les prières de la Vierge.
Et la troisième flotte ce sont les autres innombrables prières.
Toutes. Celles qui se disent à la messe et aux vêpres. Et au
salut.
Et les prières des moines qui marquent toutes les heures du
jour. Et les heures de la nuit.
Et le *Benedicite* qui se dit pour se mettre à table.
Devant une bonne soupière fumante.
Toutes, enfin toutes. Et il n'en reste plus.

the second fleet, and it is an innumerable fleet, for it is the
white sailed fleet, the innumerable fleet of *Hail Marys.*
And it is a fleet of biremes. And the first row of oars is:
Ave Maria, gratia plena;

And the second row of oars is:
Sancta Maria, mater Dei.
And all those *Hail Marys,* and all those prayers of the Virgin
and the noble *Salve Regina* are white caravels, humbly
resting under their sails on the surface of the water; like
white doves which one might take with the hand.
Now those sweet doves (resting) under their wings,
Those white familiar doves, those doves in one's hand,
Those humble doves lying on the surface of the hand,
Those doves accustomed to one's hand,
Those caravels vested with sails,
Of all ships are the most opportune,
That is, the ships which present themselves with greatest
directness in front of the port.

Such is the second fleet, the prayers of the Virgin. And the
third fleet is made up of the other innumerable prayers.
All of them. Those which are said at mass and at vespers.
And at benediction.
And the prayers of the monks which mark all the hours of
the day. And the hours of the night.

And the *Benedicite* which is said before sitting down to
meals.
Before a nice smoking soup-tureen.
All those prayers, all of them. And none are left.

Or je vois la quatrième flotte. Je vois la flotte invisible. Et ce
sont toutes les prières qui ne sont pas même dites, les
paroles qui ne sont pas prononcées.

Mais moi je les entends. Ces obscurs mouvements du cœur, les
obscurs bons mouvements, les secrets bons mouvements.

Qui jaillissent inconsciemment et qui naissent et inconsciemment montent vers moi.

Celui qui en est le siège ne les aperçoit même pas. Il n'en sait
rien, et il n'en est vraiment que le siège.

Mais moi je les recueille, dit Dieu, et je les compte et les pèse,
Parce que je suis le juge secret.

Telles sont, dit Dieu, ces trois flottes innombrables. Et la
quatrième.

Ces trois flottes visibles et cette quatrième invisible.

Ces prières secrètes dont un cœur est le siège, ces prières
secrètes du cœur. Ces mouvements secrets.

Et assailli aussi effrontément, assailli de prières et de larmes,
Directement assailli, assailli en pleine face

Après cela on veut que je les condamne. Comme c'est commode.

On veut que je les juge. On sait assez comment finissent tous
ces jugements-là et toutes ces condamnations

Un homme avait deux fils. Ça finit toujours par des embrassements.

(Et c'est encore le père qui pleure le plus).

Et par cette tendresse qui est, que je mettrais au-dessus des
Vertus même,

Parce qu'avec sa sœur la Pureté elle procède directement de
la Vierge.

Now I see the fourth fleet. I see the invisible fleet. And it is
made up of all the prayers which are not even said, the
words that are not even spoken.
But I hear them. Those obscure impulses of the heart, the
obscure and good impulses, the secret good impulses.
Which unconsciously soar up, which are born and unconsciously ascend towards me.
And he in whose breast they originate is not even aware of
them. He doesn't know about them, he is only the origi-
nator.
But I collect them, says God, and I count them and weigh
them.
Because I am the secret judge.

Such are, says God, these three innumerable fleets. And the
fourth.
These three visible fleets and this fourth invisible one.
These secret prayers originating in a heart, these secret
prayers of the heart. These secret impulses.
And being thus assailed with such effrontery, assailed with
prayers and with tears,
Directly assailed, assailed right in the face
After that I am expected to condemn them. How easy that is!
I am expected to judge them. We know well enough how all
those judgements end up and all those sentences.
A certain man had two sons. It always ends with embraces.
(And the father crying even more than anyone else).
And with that tenderness which is, which I shall always put
above the Virtues themselves.
Because with its sister Purity it proceeds directly from the
Virgin.

HEUREUX CEUX

Heureux ceux qui sont morts pour la terre charnelle,
Mais pourvu que ce fût dans une juste guerre.
Heureux ceux qui sont morts pour quatre coins de terre.
Heureux ceux qui sont morts d'une mort solennelle.

Heureux ceux qui sont morts dans les grandes batailles,
Couchés dessus le sol à la face de Dieu.
Heureux ceux qui sont morts sur un dernier haut lieu,
Parmi tout l'appareil des grandes funérailles.

Heureux ceux qui sont morts pour des cités charnelles.
Car elles sont le corps de la cité de Dieu.
Heureux ceux qui sont morts pour leur âtre et leur feu,
Et les pauvres honneurs des maisons paternelles.

Car elles sont l'image et le commencement
Et le corps et l'essai de la maison de Dieu.
Heureux ceux qui sont morts dans cet embrassement,
Dans l'étreinte d'honneur et le terrestre aveu.

BLESSED ARE

Blessed are those who died for carnal earth
Provided it was in a just war.
Blessed are those who died for a plot of ground.
Blessed are those who died a solemn death.

Blessed are those who died in great battles.
Stretched out on the ground in the face of God.
Blessed are those who died on a final high place,
Amid all the pomp of grandiose funerals.

Blessed are those who died for carnal cities.
For they are the body of the city of God.
Blessed are those who died for their hearth and their fire,
And the lowly honors of their father's house.

For such is the image and such the beginning
The body and shadow of the house of God.
Blessed are those who died in that embrace,
In honor's clasp and earth's avowal.

Car cet aveu d'honneur est le commencement
Et le premier essai d'un éternel aveu.
Heureux ceux qui sont morts dans cet écrasement,
Dans l'accomplissement de ce terrestre vœu.

Car ce vœu de la terre est le commencement
Et le premier essai d'une fidélité.
Heureux ceux qui sont morts dans ce couronnement
Et cette obéissance et cette humilité.

Heureux ceux qui sont morts, car ils sont retournés
Dans la première argile et la première terre.
Heureux ceux qui sont morts dans une juste guerre.
Heureux les épis mûrs et les blés moissonnés.

For honor's clasp is the beginning
And the first draught of eternal avowal.
Blessed are those who died in this crushing down,
In the accomplishment of this earthly vow.

For earth's vow is the beginning
And the first draught of faithfulness.
Blessed are those who died in that coronation,
In that obedience and that humility.

Blessed are those who died, for they have returned
Into primeval clay and primeval earth.
Blessed are those who died in a just war.
Blessed is the wheat that is ripe and the wheat that is gathered
    in sheaves.

EDITOR'S NOTE

It appears necessary to point out that some of Péguy's favorite expressions have taken on connotations which they did not have in the author's mind. Such words as race, fatherland, military spirit refer to realities which only lately have become perverted into dangerous slogans. Who would deny that Péguy was French to the marrow, that he was proud to belong to his race, as he was proud of his family. But who, also, would deny that he took his place humbly in the universal structure made of many races, and was conscious of more than one spiritual heritage? No fascist could have written, as Péguy did: 'I do not say that we are worth more than the others. We belong to one race, they belong to another race. We are men. We are sinners.'

The title and subtitles are not Péguy's. Omissions in the text are indicated by dashes. The whole text is quoted from Charles Péguy's 'Cahiers de la Quinzaine', Paris 1900–1914. Therefore the dates of quotations refer to their first publication. The roman numerals indicate the Series numbers of the 'Cahiers', the arabic numerals indicate the number of the issue. Spelling and punctuation correspond to the text of the 'Cahiers'. The appreciations are quoted from the following books:

E. Mounier, La pensée de Ch. Péguy, Paris 1931, p. viii.
Cardinal Verdier in: Péguy, Pensées, Paris 1930, p. 8
André Gide, Nouveaux Prétextes, Paris 1930, pp. 213-215
Henri Bergson in: Tharaud, Notre cher Péguy, Paris 1926, I, p. 265
J. & J. Tharaud, Notre cher Péguy, I, p. 19, and II, p. 187.
M. Barrès, Péguy, Oeuvres compl. Paris 1920, vol. II, p. 34
A. Béguin in: Neue Schweizerische Rundschau, Mai 1941
G. N. Shuster, Catholic church and current literature, London 1930, p. 82
Pierre Péguy in: Péguy, Prières, Paris 1934, p. 16

LES VERITES FONDAMENTALES   PAGE

LE MONDE MODERNE